Elizabeth Hartman

Patchwork City

75 Innovative Blocks for the Modern Quilter • 6 Sampler Quilts

stashBOOKS.

an imprint of C&T Publishing

Text copyright © 2014 by Elizabeth Hartman

Photography and Artwork copyright © 2014 by C&T Publishing, Inc.

PUBLISHER: Amy Marson

CREATIVE DIRECTOR: Gailen Runge

ART DIRECTOR: Kristy Zacharias

EDITOR: Liz Aneloski

TECHNICAL EDITORS: Doreen Hazel and Gailen Runge

COVER/BOOK DESIGNER: April Mostek

PRODUCTION COORDINATOR: Rue Flaherty

PRODUCTION EDITOR: Joanna Burgarino

ILLUSTRATOR: Jessica Jenkins

PHOTO ASSISTANT: Mary Peyton Peppo

STYLED PHOTOGRAPHY by Nissa Brehmer and
INSTRUCTIONAL PHOTOGRAPHY by Diane Pedersen, unless otherwise noted

Published by Stash Books, an imprint of C&T Publishing, Inc., P.O. Box 1456,
Lafayette, CA 94549

Library of Congress Cataloging-in-Publication Data

Hartman, Elizabeth (Elizabeth Anne)

 Patchwork city : 75 innovative blocks for the modern quilter : 6 sampler quilts / Elizabeth
Hartman.

      pages cm

 Includes index.

 ISBN 978-1-60705-951-6 (soft cover)

 1. Patchwork--Patterns. 2. Machine quilting--Patterns. 3. Patchwork quilts. I. Title.

 TT835.H34219 2014

 746.46--dc23

                                2014017514

Printed in China

10 9 8 7 6 5 4 3 2 1

Contents

Acknowledgments

This book is a project I've wanted to do for the past several years, and it has been wonderful to see it come to life! *Patchwork City* would not have been possible without the help and support of my friends and family. Thank you, in particular, to Violet Craft, Jen Carlton Bailly, Monica Solorio Snow, Amber Wilson, and Jaime Young. You're all amazing, and I'll never be able to thank you enough for all the ways you helped me during the production of this book.

I also want to thank my favorite local fabric shops: Bolt, Cool Cottons, and Modern Domestic. We're so lucky to have such fabulous shops in Portland!

Thank you, Krista Withers, for the beautiful longarm quilting on *Uptown* (page 165). All other sewing and quilting was done by me on my Janome 1600P-QC.

Thank you to Robert Kaufman Fabrics for providing Kona Cotton and Essex Linen solids for the quilts in this book, and to Michael Miller Fabrics for providing print fabrics for the *Uptown* quilt.

Introduction

Like so many quilters, I find inspiration for quilt designs wherever I go. The side of a building, a stack of dishes in the cupboard—everything seems to have the potential to be a beautiful quilt block.

I also love fabric—prints and solids, brights and neutrals. It often seems like I have more fabric than I will ever be able to turn into projects!

It was this feeling of being overwhelmed by possibility that led me to write a book of sampler quilts.

The 75 blocks in this book were inspired by the places and everyday objects I see around me. As I built more and more blocks, they became a kind of patchwork city—a reflection of the shapes, colors, and fabrics I love.

Making a sampler quilt is a long-term project, and I encourage you to embrace that fact. We all have projects that need to be completed on a deadline, but this should not be one of them. Embrace the idea of making a quilt that is for you and is a reflection of your favorite things. Consider each block as its own composition and take the time to choose fabric thoughtfully. It will take as long as it needs to. Build your very own patchwork city!

What Is a Sampler Quilt?

A sampler quilt includes one each of a variety of blocks, rather than a single block repeated across the entire quilt. Quilters have historically made samplers to practice and display a variety of skills.

About This Book

Patchwork City includes 75 block patterns: 25 each in three sizes (8″ × 8″, 5″ × 8″, and 5″ × 14″). The instructions for each block are written as individual projects, making them perfect for using scrap fabric. Don't hesitate to skip around in the book to mix and match your favorites!

I've also included six projects that allow you to combine the blocks to make sampler quilts. Each of the quilt projects includes yardage requirements for sashing, backing, and binding.

The How-To chapter (page 183) includes the basics of making the blocks. More in-depth information about how to sandwich, quilt, and bind your project can be found in my other books, *The Practical Guide to Patchwork* and *Modern Patchwork*.

Block Patterns

Block Index

8″ × 8″ Blocks

The blocks in this section will measure 8½″ × 8½″ including a ¼″ seam allowance on each side. Once they are sewn into a project, the finished blocks will measure 8″ × 8″.

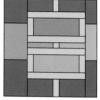
Apartment, page 46

Clock Tower, page 56

Crosswalk, page 14

Donut Shop, page 12

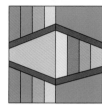
Drawbridge, page 44

Duplex, page 36

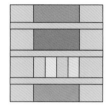
Elevator, page 32

Favorite Sweater, page 26

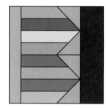
Fence, page 30

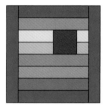
Food Truck, page 54

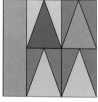
Forest Park, page 10

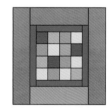
Intercom, page 16

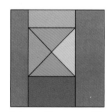
Intersection, page 18

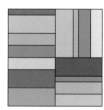
Library, page 40

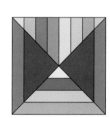
Lobby, page 58

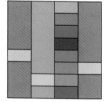
Mini Storage, page 24

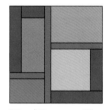
Mixed Use, page 50

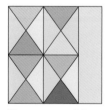
Museum, page 34

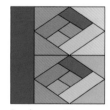
Porch, page 22

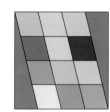
River Walk, page 48

Roadblock, page 52

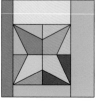
Spotlight, page 38

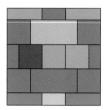
Streetlight, page 42

Sushi, page 28

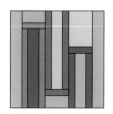
Transit Center, page 20

5″ × 8″ Blocks

The blocks in this section will measure 5½″ × 8½″ including a ¼″ seam allowance on each side. Once they are sewn into a project, the finished blocks will measure 5″ × 8″.

Airport, page 106

Bowling Alley, page 92

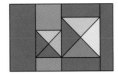
Emergency Exit, page 72

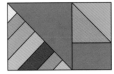
Fortune Cookies, page 104

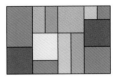
Half Sandwich, page 62

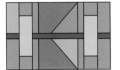
House Plant, page 74

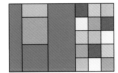
Karaoke, page 94

Kiosk, page 82

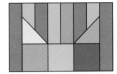
Magazine Rack, page 80

Meow, page 78

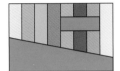
Onramp, page 66

Parking Garage, page 60

Parking Meters, page 84

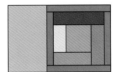
Planter Box, page 68

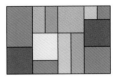
Raindrops, page 98

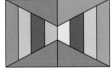
Rec Center, page 64

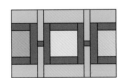
Rose Garden, page 88

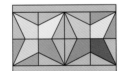
Sequins, page 70

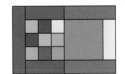
Sidewalk, page 102

Skyline, page 108

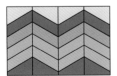
Stripey Socks, page 100

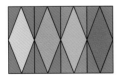
Supermarket, page 90

Traffic Cones, page 96

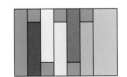
Turnstile, page 86

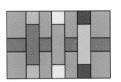
Waterfront, page 76

5˝ × 14˝ Blocks

The blocks in this section will measure 5½˝ × 14½˝ including a ¼˝ seam allowance on each side. Once they are sewn into a project, the finished blocks will measure 5˝ × 14˝.

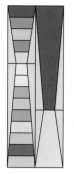
Auditorium, page 134

Balcony, page 150

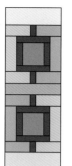
Bookstore, page 130

Brewery, page 114

Carpool, page 116

City Hall, page 110

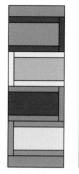
Coffee Shop, page 122

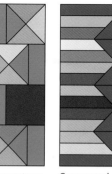
Cornerstone, page 140

Corrugated Cardboard, page 146

Do Not Enter, page 158

Dog Park, page 118

Escalator, page 120

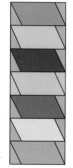
Haircut, page 124

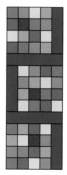
Laundromat, page 156

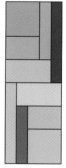
Look Both Ways, page 132

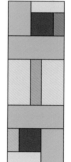
Post Office Box, page 136

Puddles, page 152

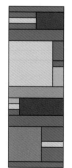
Restaurant, page 144

Skylight, page 126

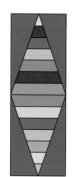
Stadium, page 142

Storefront, page 128

Tiki Bar, page 148

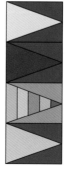
Tow-Away Zone, page 154

Window Washer, page 138

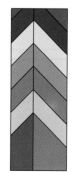
Zoo Train, page 112

Using the Block Patterns

The blocks in this book can be made using whatever combination of fabrics your imagination can devise. I've provided three examples for each block using different fabrics, but that's really only the tip of the iceberg in terms of the possibilities. You may find that you want to emulate some of my fabric choices, you may want to use them as jumping-off points, or you may want to ignore them entirely. The most important thing is to have fun and express yourself with fabric!

Each of the block designs includes a diagram that has the pieces of the block labeled with a letter or letter/number combination, and a corresponding chart detailing the size and required quantity of each rotary-cut piece. Use the diagrams and charts to determine how much fabric you will need in order to make each block. Some of the blocks use one or more freezer-paper templates; full-size patterns for these templates can be found on the pattern pullout sheets.

The cutting charts for each block design include columns labeled "Size to Cut" and "Trim Using." For many pieces, the entry in the "Size to Cut" column is just that—the exact size of the rotary-cut piece. Whenever the "Trim Using" column is blank, the dimensions in the "Size to Cut" column represent the exact size needed.

For blocks using template pieces, you will find dimensions in the "Size to Cut" column and a pattern number in the "Trim Using" column. That means that, for example, for the Forest Park block (page 10), piece A should be cut using Template A from Pattern 1 and that a 4″ × 5¼″ piece of fabric should be large enough for the task. In these cases, the information in the "Size to Cut" column is simply intended as a helpful reference. You may find that you're able to squeeze a template shape onto a smaller or oddly shaped scrap of fabric. If you're fussy cutting (see Fussy Cutting, page 185) or shortcut piecing (see Shortcut Piecing, page 189) you may find that you need slightly larger pieces of fabric than what is listed in the "Size to Cut" column.

Forest Park

Fabric Requirements and Cutting

Piece	Number to Cut	Size to Cut	Trim Using
A	4	4″ × 5¼″	Template A— Pattern 1
B1	1	2½″ × 5¾″	Template B1— Pattern 1
B2	1	2½″ × 5¾″	Template B2— Pattern 1
C1	3	2½″ × 5¾″	Template C1— Pattern 1
C2	3	2½″ × 5¾″	Template C2— Pattern 1
D	1	2½″ × 8½″	

All seams are sewn with a ¼″ seam allowance and pressed open.

NOTE

Most of the pieces in this block are cut using templates from Pattern 1 (pullout page P1). The dimensions listed in the chart under "Size to Cut" represent the amount of fabric required for each piece. More fabric may be required for shortcut piecing (page 189) or fussy cutting (page 185).

To make a template from a pattern, refer to Making and Using Freezer-Paper Templates (pages 186 and 187). When cutting your fabric, remember to add seam allowances and mark points for matching seams.

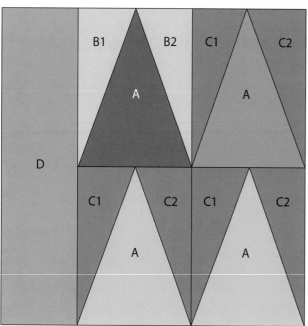

Make the Block

Make the Contrasting Triangle Unit

Sew piece B1 and piece B2 to a piece A. The unit will now be 3½″ × 4½″. *figure a*

Make the Triangle Units

1. Sew a piece C1 and a piece C2 to a piece A. *figure b*

2. Repeat Step 1 to create a total of 3 triangle units AC, each 3½″ × 4½″.

Finish the Block

1. Arrange the 4 triangle units in 2 rows, placing the contrasting triangle unit at the top left. Sew the units in each row together. Then sew the 2 rows together.

2. Sew piece D to the left side of the block. *figure c*

figure a figure b

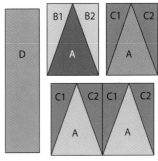

figure c

ALTERNATE IDEAS

Donut Shop

Fabric Requirements and Cutting

Piece	Number to Cut	Size to Cut
A	1	2½″ × 2½″
B	1	1½″ × 2½″
C	1	1½″ × 3½″
D	1	2½″ × 3½″
E	1	2½″ × 5½″
F	1	2½″ × 5½″
G	1	2½″ × 7½″
H	1	1½″ × 7½″
I	1	1½″ × 8½″

All seams are sewn with a ¼″ seam allowance and pressed open.

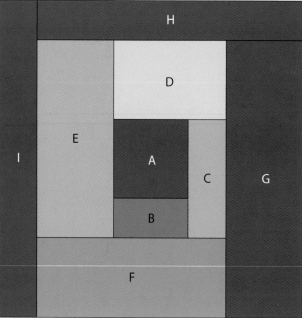

Make the Block

Sew the Inner Ring

1. Sew piece B to the bottom of piece A.

2. Sew piece C to the right side of the block.

3. Sew piece D to the top of the block.

4. Sew piece E to the left side of the block. *figure a*

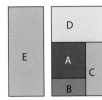
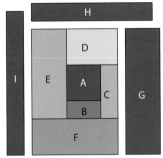

figure a

Add the Background Ring

1. Sew piece F to the bottom of the block.

2. Sew piece G to the right side of the block.

3. Sew piece H to the top of the block.

4. Sew piece I to the left side of the block. *figure b*

figure b

ALTERNATE IDEAS

Crosswalk

Fabric Requirements and Cutting

Piece	Number to Cut	Size to Cut
A	4	1½˝ × 6½˝
B	3	1˝ × 6½˝
C	2	1¾˝ × 6½˝
D	2	1½˝ × 8½˝

All seams are sewn with a ¼˝ seam allowance and pressed open.

Make the Block

1. Beginning with a piece A, sew the pieces A and B together in alternating order.

2. Sew pieces C to the top and bottom of the block.

3. Sew pieces D to the left and right sides of the block.

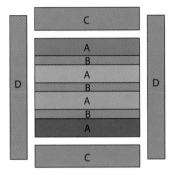

ALTERNATE IDEAS

Intercom

Fabric Requirements and Cutting

Piece	Number to Cut	Size to Cut
A	15	1½″ × 1½″
B	1	1½″ × 1½″
C	2	1″ × 4½″
D	2	1″ × 5½″
E	2	2″ × 5½″
F	2	2″ × 8½″

All seams are sewn with a ¼″ seam allowance and pressed open.

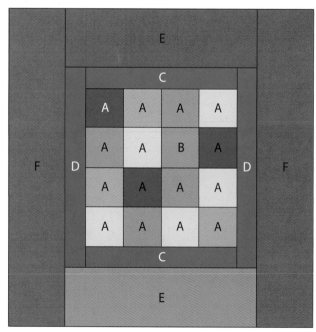

Make the Block

Sew the Tiles Together

1. Arrange the pieces A and B in 4 rows of 4 each, placing piece B third from the left in the second row.

2. Sew the pieces in each row together. Then sew the rows together to create a 16-patch formation. *figure a*

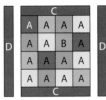

figure a   figure b

Add the Inner Ring

1. Sew pieces C to the top and bottom of the block.

2. Sew pieces D to the left and right sides of the block. *figure b*

Add the Background Ring

1. Sew pieces E to the top and bottom of the block.

2. Sew pieces F to the left and right sides of the block. *figure c*

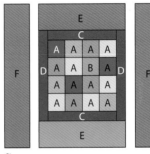

figure c

ALTERNATE IDEAS

Intersection

Fabric Requirements and Cutting

Piece	Number to Cut	Size to Cut	Trim Using
A1	2	3″ × 5½″	Template A1—Pattern 2
A2	2	3″ × 5½″	Template A2—Pattern 2
B	1	2″ × 4½″	
C	1	3″ × 4½″	
D	1	2″ × 8½″	
E	1	3″ × 8½″	

All seams are sewn with a ¼″ seam allowance and pressed open.

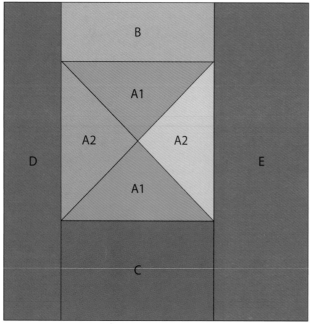

NOTE

Some of the pieces in this block are cut using templates from Pattern 2 (pullout page P2). The dimensions listed in the chart under "Size to Cut" represent the amount of fabric required for each piece. More fabric may be required for shortcut piecing (page 189) or fussy cutting (page 185).

To make a template from a pattern, refer to Making and Using Freezer-Paper Templates (pages 186 and 187). When cutting your fabric, remember to add seam allowances and mark points for matching seams.

Make the Block

Make the Hourglass Unit

1. Sew together piece A1 and piece A2. Repeat with the remaining pieces A1 and A2.

2. Sew the pairs together to create the 4½″ × 4½″ hourglass unit. *figure a*

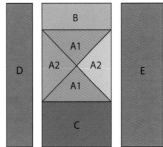

figure a

Make the Vertical Stripe

1. Sew piece B to the top of the hourglass unit.

2. Sew piece C to the bottom of the hourglass unit.

Finish the Block

1. Sew piece D to the left side of the block.

2. Sew piece E to the right side of the block. *figure b*

figure b

ALTERNATE IDEAS _____

Transit Center

Fabric Requirements and Cutting

Piece	Number to Cut	Size to Cut
A	2	1½″ × 7″
B	4	1″ × 7″
C	3	1″ × 2½″
D	1	1½″ × 5″
E	2	1″ × 5″
F	2	1½″ × 2½″
G	1	2½″ × 3½″
H	2	1½″ × 8½″

All seams are sewn with a ¼″ seam allowance and pressed open.

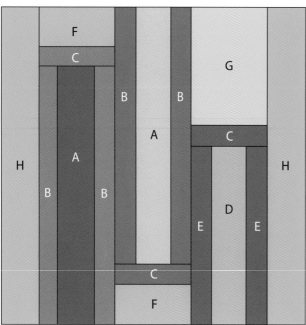

Make the Block

Make Column 1

1. Sew pieces B to the left and right sides of a piece A.

2. Sew a piece C to the top of unit AB.

3. Sew a piece F to the top to finish column 1. *figure a*

Make Column 2

1. Sew pieces B to the left and right sides of the remaining piece A.

2. Sew a piece C to the bottom of unit AB.

3. Sew the remaining piece F to the bottom to finish column 2. *figure b*

Make Column 3

1. Sew pieces E to the left and right sides of piece D.

2. Sew the remaining piece C to the top of unit DE.

3. Sew piece G to the top to finish column 3. *figure c*

Finish the Block

1. Sew the columns together.

2. Sew pieces H to the left and right sides of the block. *figure d*

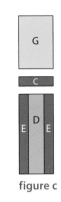

figure a   figure b   figure c

figure d

ALTERNATE IDEAS

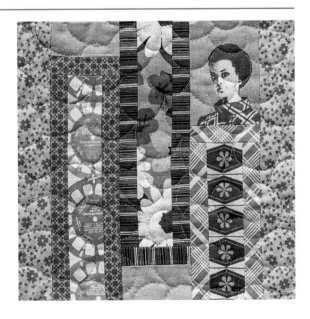

Porch

Fabric Requirements and Cutting

Piece	Number to Cut	Size to Cut	Trim Using
A	2	2″ × 3″	Template A—Pattern 3
B	2	2″ × 2¾″	Template B—Pattern 3
C	2	2″ × 4″	Template C—Pattern 3
D	2	2″ × 4″	Template D—Pattern 3
E	2	2″ × 5¼″	Template E—Pattern 3
F1	4	3″ × 4¼″	Template F1—Pattern 3
F2	4	3″ × 4¼″	Template F2—Pattern 3
G	1	2½″ × 8½″	

All seams are sewn with a ¼″ seam allowance and pressed open.

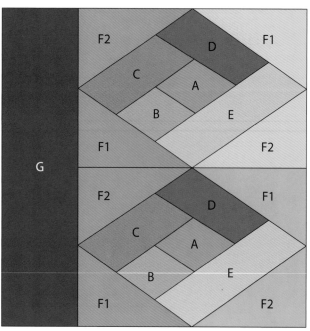

NOTE

Most of the pieces in this block are cut using templates from Pattern 3 (pullout page P1). The dimensions listed in the chart under "Size to Cut" represent the amount of fabric required for each piece. More fabric may be required for shortcut piecing (page 189) or fussy cutting (page 185).

To make a template from a pattern, refer to Making and Using Freezer-Paper Templates (pages 186 and 187). When cutting your fabric, remember to add seam allowances and mark points for matching seams.

Make the Block

Make the Diamond Units

1. Sew 1 each of pieces B, C, D, and E around a piece A. (This will be a lot like making a Log Cabin block, but with slightly different shapes.) *figure a*

2. Sew corner pieces F1 and F2 to the diamond to make a unit 4½″ × 6½″. *figure b*

3. Repeat Steps 1 and 2 to make a second diamond unit.

Finish the Block

1. Sew together the 2 diamond units.

2. Sew piece G to the left side of the block. *figure c*

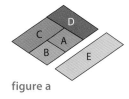

figure a

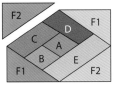

figure b

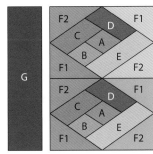

figure c

ALTERNATE IDEAS

Mini Storage

Fabric Requirements and Cutting

Piece	Number to Cut	Size to Cut
A	4	1½″ × 2½″
B	1	2½″ × 4½″
C	1	2½″ × 3½″
D	1	2½″ × 6½″
E	1	1½″ × 2½″
F	7	1½″ × 2½″
G	1	2½″ × 5½″
H	1	2½″ × 2½″

All seams are sewn with a ¼″ seam allowance and pressed open.

Make the Block

Make Column 1

Sew piece B to the top of a piece A, and piece C to the bottom. *figure a*

Make Column 2

Sew piece D to the top of a piece A, and piece E to the bottom. *figure b*

Make Column 3

Sew all the pieces F and a piece A in a column, with piece A second from the top. *figure c*

Make Column 4

Sew piece G to the top of the remaining piece A, and piece H to the bottom. *figure d*

Finish the Block

Sew the columns together. *figure e*

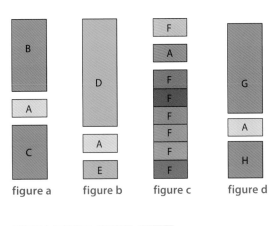

figure a   figure b   figure c   figure d

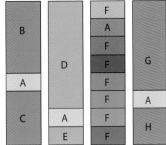

figure e

ALTERNATE IDEAS

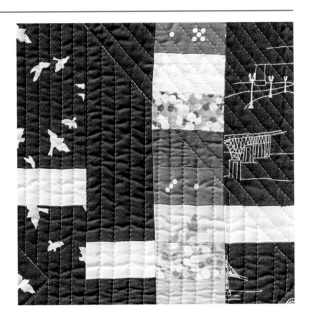

Favorite Sweater

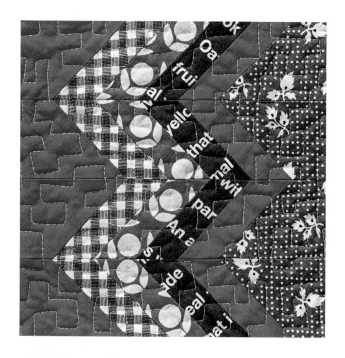

Fabric Requirements and Cutting

Piece	Number to Cut	Size to Cut
A	2	3½″ × 10″
B	2	1¼″ × 10″
C	2	1¼″ × 10″
D	2	1¼″ × 10″
E	2	1¼″ × 10″
F	2	3½″ × 10″

All seams are sewn with a ¼″ seam allowance and pressed open.

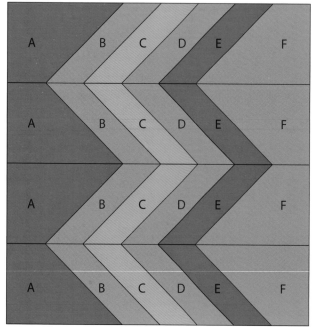

NOTE

Each stripe requires 2 pieces of fabric. If you want the look of continuous stripes, use 2 pieces of the same fabric for each stripe.

Make the Block

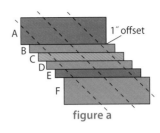

figure a

Make Rows 1 and 3

1. Beginning with piece A at the top, arrange each of pieces A, B, C, D, E, and F alphabetically in a column. Sew the pieces together, aligning each piece 1˝ to the right of the piece above it, to create a pieced stack that leans to the left.

2. Use the 45° markings on your ruler to cut 2 pieced strips, each 2½˝ wide. These will become rows 1 and 3. *figure a*

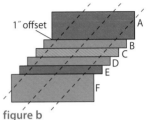

figure b

Make Rows 2 and 4

1. Beginning with piece A at the top, arrange each of pieces A, B, C, D, E, and F alphabetically in a column. Sew the pieces together, aligning each piece 1˝ to the left of the piece above it, to create a pieced stack that leans to the right.

2. Use the 45° markings on your ruler to cut 2 pieced strips, each 2½˝ wide. These will become rows 2 and 4. *figure b*

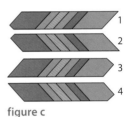

figure c

Finish the Block

1. Sew together rows 1, 2, 3, and 4, matching the seams between the stripes.

2. Trim away the excess fabric from the sides to make a block 8½˝ × 8½˝. *figures c & d*

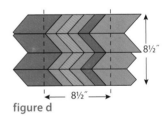

figure d

ALTERNATE IDEAS

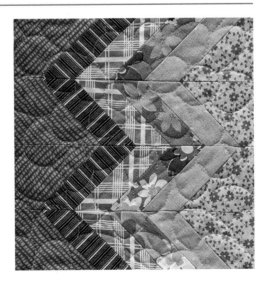

Sushi

Fabric Requirements and Cutting

Piece	Number to Cut	Size to Cut	Trim Using
A	2	3″ × 4″	Template A—Pattern 4
B	2	3″ × 5″	Template B—Pattern 4
C	2	3″ × 4″	Template C—Pattern 4
D	2	3″ × 4″	Template D—Pattern 4
E	2	3″ × 5″	Template E—Pattern 4
F	2	3″ × 4″	Template F—Pattern 4

All seams are sewn with a ¼″ seam allowance and pressed open.

NOTE

All the pieces for this block will be cut using templates from Pattern 4 (pullout page P1). The dimensions listed in the chart under "Size to Cut" represent the amount of fabric required for each piece. More fabric may be required for shortcut piecing (page 189) or fussy cutting (page 185).

To make a template from a pattern, refer to Making and Using Freezer-Paper Templates (pages 186 and 187). When cutting your fabric, remember to add seam allowances and mark points for matching seams.

Make the Block

Make the Top Half

1. Sew a piece A to the left side of a piece B.

2. Sew a piece C to the right side of piece B to finish row 1.

3. Sew a piece D to the left side of a piece E.

4. Sew a piece F to the right side of piece E to finish row 2.

5. Sew together rows 1 and 2. *figure a*

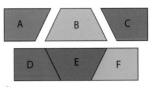

figure a

Make the Bottom Half

Repeat Steps 1–5 (above) to make the bottom half. *figure b*

figure b

Finish the Block

Sew the top and bottom halves together. *figure c*

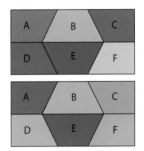

figure c

ALTERNATE IDEAS

Fence

Fabric Requirements and Cutting

Piece	Number to Cut	Size to Cut
A	8	1½″ × 5½″
B	4	2½″ × 2½″
C	1	1½″ × 8½″
D	1	2½″ × 8½″

All seams are sewn with a ¼″ seam allowance and pressed open.

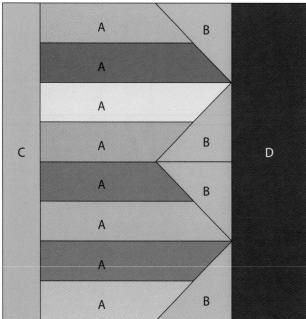

——— SEWING DIAGONAL SEAMS ———

Align the 2 pieces of fabric with right sides together. Use a fabric marker to draw the diagonal seam line as shown in the diagram. Sew along the marked line. Trim away the excess fabric to leave a ¼″ seam allowance. Press the seam open.

Make the Block

Make the Stripe Units

For Steps 2 and 3, refer to Sewing Diagonal Seams (page 30).

1. Sew together 4 pieces A. *figure a*

2. Place a piece B on top of a unit A. Mark and sew the diagonal seam. *figure b*

3. Place a second piece B on top of the unit A. Mark and sew the diagonal seam. *figure c*

4. Repeat Steps 1–3 to make a second stripe unit AB.

Finish the Block

1. Sew the 2 stripe units together.

2. Sew piece C to the left side of the block.

3. Sew piece D to the right side of the block. *figure d*

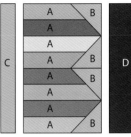

figure a

figure b

figure c

figure d

ALTERNATE IDEAS

SPRING/ SUMMER 2005

Elevator

Fabric Requirements and Cutting

Piece	Number to Cut	Size to Cut
A	2	2″ × 4½″
B	1	2¼″ × 4½″
C	4	1½″ × 2¼″
D	3	1″ × 8½″
E	4	2″ × 2½″
F	4	2¼″ × 2½″

All seams are sewn with a ¼″ seam allowance and pressed open.

Make the Block

Make Rows 1 and 4

1. Sew pieces E to the left and right sides of a piece A to make row 1.

2. Repeat Step 1 to make row 4. *figure a*

Make Row 2

Sew pieces F to the left and right sides of piece B to make row 2. *figure b*

Make Row 3

1. Sew together the 4 pieces C.

2. Sew pieces F to the left and right sides of pieced unit C to make row 3. *figure c*

Finish the Block

Sew the 4 rows together, sewing pieces D between the rows. *figure d*

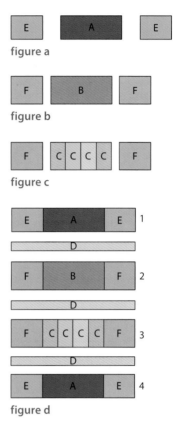

figure a

figure b

figure c

figure d

ALTERNATE IDEAS

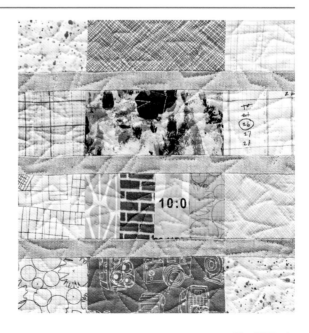

Museum

Fabric Requirements and Cutting

Piece	Number to Cut	Size to Cut	Trim Using
A	4	3″ × 4¼″	Template A— Pattern 5
B	4	2¼″ × 5¾″	Template B— Pattern 5
C	4	3″ × 4¼″	Template C— Pattern 5
D	4	2¼″ × 5¾″	Template D— Pattern 5
E	1	2½″ × 8½″	

All seams are sewn with a ¼″ seam allowance and pressed open.

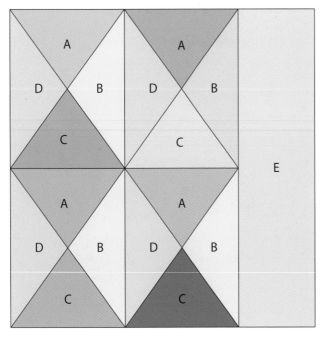

NOTE

Most of the pieces in this block are cut using templates from Pattern 5 (pullout page P1). The dimensions listed in the chart under "Size to Cut" represent the amount of fabric required for each piece. More fabric may be required for shortcut piecing (page 189) or fussy cutting (page 185).

To make a template from a pattern, refer to Making and Using Freezer-Paper Templates (pages 186 and 187). When cutting your fabric, remember to add seam allowances and mark points for matching seams.

Make the Block

Make the Hourglass Units

1. Sew a piece A to a piece B.

2. Sew a piece C to a piece D.

3. Sew the triangle pairs together to create an hourglass unit, 3½″ × 4½″.

4. Repeat Steps 1–3 to make a total of 4 hourglass units. *figure a*

figure a

Finish the Block

1. Arrange and sew the hourglass units into 2 rows of 2 units each.

2. Sew the 2 rows together.

3. Sew piece E to the right side of the block. *figure b*

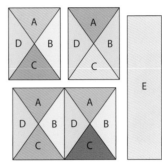

figure b

ALTERNATE IDEAS

Duplex

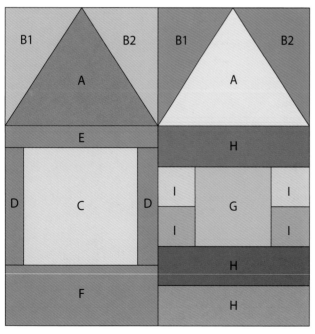

Fabric Requirements and Cutting

Piece	Number to Cut	Size to Cut	Trim Using
A	2	4″ × 5″	Template A— Pattern 6
B1	2	3″ × 4″	Template B1— Pattern 6
B2	2	3″ × 4″	Template B2— Pattern 6
C	1	3½″ × 3½″	
D	2	1″ × 3½″	
E	1	1″ × 4½″	
F	1	2″ × 4½″	
G	1	2½″ × 2½″	
H	3	1½″ × 4½″	
I	4	1½″ × 1½″	

All seams are sewn with a ¼″ seam allowance and pressed open.

NOTE

Some of the pieces in this block are cut using templates from Pattern 6 (pullout page P1). The dimensions listed in the chart under "Size to Cut" represent the amount of fabric required for each piece. More fabric may be required for shortcut piecing (page 189) or fussy cutting (page 185).

To make a template from a pattern, refer to Making and Using Freezer-Paper Templates (pages 186 and 187). When cutting your fabric, remember to add seam allowances and mark points for matching seams.

Make the Block

Make the Roofs

1. Sew a piece B1 to the left side of a piece A.

2. Sew a piece B2 to the right side to complete a roof unit, 3½″ × 4½″.

3. Repeat Steps 1 and 2 to make a second roof unit. *figure a*

Make Column 1

1. Sew pieces D to the left and right sides of piece C.

2. Sew piece E to the top of unit CD, and piece F to the bottom.

3. Sew a roof unit to the top to complete column 1. *figure b*

Make Column 2

1. Sew together 2 pieces I. Sew together the remaining pieces I.

2. Sew the pieced units I to the left and right sides of piece G.

3. Sew pieces H to the top and bottom of unit GI. Sew the remaining piece H to the bottom.

4. Sew the remaining roof unit to the top to complete column 2. *figure c*

Finish the Block

Sew together column 1 and column 2. *figure d*

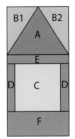

figure a

figure b

figure c

figure d

ALTERNATE IDEAS

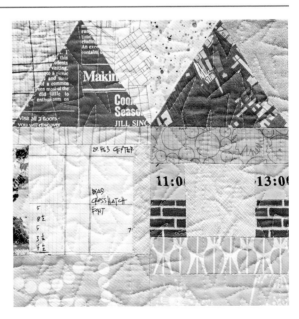

Spotlight

Fabric Requirements and Cutting

Piece	Number to Cut	Size to Cut	Trim Using
A	4	2½″ × 4¼″	Template A— Pattern 7
B1	4	2¼″ × 4″	Template B1— Pattern 7
B2	4	2¼″ × 4″	Template B2— Pattern 7
C	1	2½″ × 5½″	
D	1	1½″ × 5½″	
E	1	1½″ × 8½″	
F	1	2½″ × 8½″	

All seams are sewn with a ¼″ seam allowance and pressed open.

─────────── **NOTE** ───────────

Some of the pieces in this block are cut using templates from Pattern 7 (pullout page P1). The dimensions listed in the chart under "Size to Cut" represent the amount of fabric required for each piece. More fabric may be required for shortcut piecing (page 189) or fussy cutting (page 185).

To make a template from a pattern, refer to Making and Using Freezer-Paper Templates (pages 186 and 187). When cutting your fabric, remember to add seam allowances and mark points for matching seams.

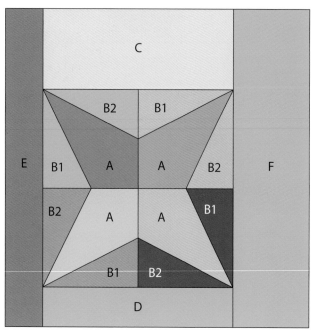

Make the Block

Make the Star

1. Sew a piece B1 to the left side of a piece A.

2. Sew a piece B2 to the right side of piece A.

3. Repeat Steps 1 and 2 to create a total of 4 units AB, each 3″ × 3″. *figure a*

4. Arrange and sew the 4 pieced points into 2 rows of 2 each. *figure b*

5. Sew the rows together to complete the star.

Finish the Block

1. Sew piece C to the top of the star unit, and piece D to the bottom.

2. Sew piece E to the left side of the star unit, and piece F to the right side. *figure c*

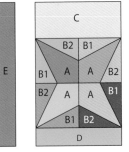

figure a   figure b

figure c

ALTERNATE IDEAS

Library

Fabric Requirements and Cutting

Piece	Number to Cut	Size to Cut
A	3	1˝ × 4½˝
B	5	2˝ × 4½˝
C	7	1½˝ × 4½˝

All seams are sewn with a ¼˝ seam allowance and pressed open.

Make the Block

Make Column 1

Arrange pieces A, B, and C in a column and sew together. *figure a*

Make Column 2

1. Sew together pieces A, B, and C for the upper half. *figure b*

2. Sew together the remaining pieces A, B, and C for the lower half. *figure c*

3. Sew together the upper and lower halves to complete column 2.

Finish the Block

Sew together column 1 and column 2. *figure d*

figure b

figure c

figure a

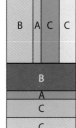

figure d

ALTERNATE IDEAS

Streetlight

Fabric Requirements and Cutting

Piece	Number to Cut	Size to Cut
A	2	1½″ × 2½″
B	2	2½″ × 4½″
C	2	2½″ × 2½″
D	4	1½″ × 3½″
E	5	2½″ × 2½″
F	2	1½″ × 2½″

All seams are sewn with a ¼″ seam allowance and pressed open.

Make the Block

Make Row 1 and Row 5

Sew pieces D to the left and right sides of a piece A to make row 1. Repeat to make row 5. *figure a*

Make Row 2 and Row 4

Sew pieces E to the left and right sides of a piece B to make row 2. Repeat to make row 4. *figure b*

Make Row 3

1. Sew pieces C to the left and right sides of the remaining piece E.

2. Sew pieces F to the left and right sides of unit CE to make row 3. *figure c*

Finish the Block

Sew together the 5 rows. *figure d*

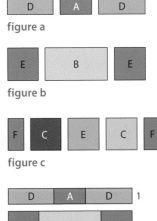

figure a

figure b

figure c

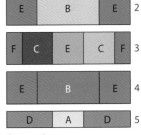

figure d

ALTERNATE IDEAS

Drawbridge

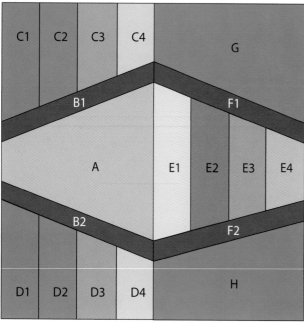

Fabric Requirements and Cutting

Piece	Number to Cut	Size to Cut	Trim Using
A	1	5″ × 5″	Template A—Pattern 8
B1	1	1½″ × 5½″	Template B1—Pattern 8
B2	1	1½″ × 5½″	Template B2—Pattern 8
C1	1	1½″ × 4″	
C2	1	1½″ × 3½″	
C3	1	1½″ × 3¼″	
C4	1	1½″ × 2¾″	
D1	1	1½″ × 4″	
D2	1	1½″ × 3½″	
D3	1	1½″ × 3¼″	
D4	1	1½″ × 2¾″	
E1	1	1½″ × 6″	
E2	1	1½″ × 4¼″	
E3	1	1½″ × 3½″	
E4	1	1½″ × 2¾″	
F1	1	1½″ × 5½″	Template F1—Pattern 9
F2	1	1½″ × 5½″	Template F2—Pattern 9
G	1	4″ × 5″	Template G—Pattern 9
H	1	4″ × 5″	Template H—Pattern 9

All seams are sewn with a ¼″ seam allowance and pressed open.

—————— **NOTE** ——————

Some of the pieces in this block are cut using templates from Patterns 8 and 9 (pullout page P1). The dimensions listed in the chart under "Size to Cut" represent the amount of fabric required for each piece. More fabric may be required for shortcut piecing (page 189) or fussy cutting (page 185).

To make a template from a pattern, refer to Making and Using Freezer-Paper Templates (pages 186 and 187). When cutting your fabric, remember to add seam allowances and mark points for matching seams.

Make the Block

Make the Left Side

1. Sew pieces C1–C4 together, aligning the pieces at the top. *figure a*

2. Use Template C from Pattern 8 to cut unit C from the pieced unit. *figure a*

3. Sew pieces D1–D4 together, aligning the pieces at the bottom. *figure b*

4. Use Template D from Pattern 8 to cut unit D from the pieced unit. *figure b*

5. Sew piece B1 and piece B2 to piece A. *figure d*

6. Sew unit C and unit D to unit AB. *figure d*

Make the Right Side

1. Sew pieces E1–E4 together. *figure c*

2. Use Template E from Pattern 9 to cut unit E from the pieced unit. *figure c*

3. Sew piece F1 and piece F2 to unit E. *figure d*

4. Sew piece G and piece H to unit EF. *figure d*

Finish the Block

Sew together the left and right sides. *figure d*

figure a   figure b   figure c

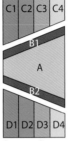 

figure d

ALTERNATE IDEAS

Apartment

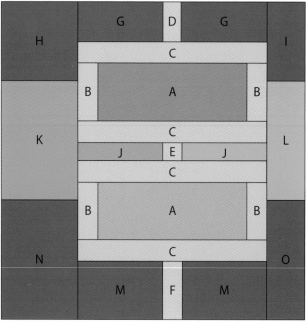

Fabric Requirements and Cutting

Piece	Number to Cut	Size to Cut
A	2	2″ × 4½″
B	4	1″ × 2″
C	4	1″ × 5½″
D	1	1″ × 1½″
E	1	1″ × 1″
F	1	1″ × 2″
G	2	1½″ × 2¾″
H	1	2½″ × 2½″
I	1	1½″ × 2½″
J	2	1″ × 2¾″
K	1	2½″ × 3½″
L	1	1½″ × 3½″
M	2	2″ × 2¾″
N	1	2½″ × 3½″
O	1	1½″ × 3½″

All seams are sewn with a ¼″ seam allowance and pressed open.

Make the Block

Make Columns 1 and 3

1. Sew pieces H and N to piece K. *figure a*

2. Sew pieces I and O to piece L. *figure b*

Make Column 2

1. Sew a piece B to both sides of each piece A.

2. Sew a piece C to the top and bottom of each unit AB. *figure c*

3. Sew pieces G to piece D. *figure d*

4. Sew pieces J to piece E. *figure e*

5. Sew pieces M to piece F. *figure f*

6. Sew the 5 pieced units together. *figure g*

Finish the Block

Sew together columns 1, 2, and 3. *figure h*

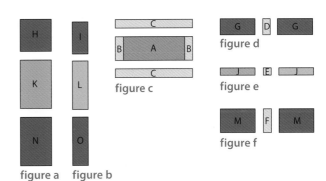

figure a   figure b

figure c

figure d

figure e

figure f

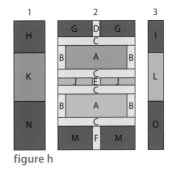

figure g

figure h

ALTERNATE IDEAS

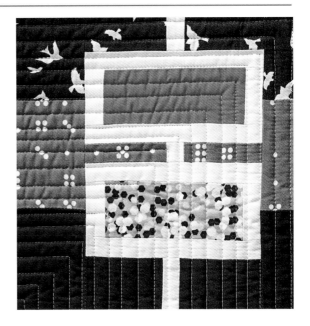

River Walk

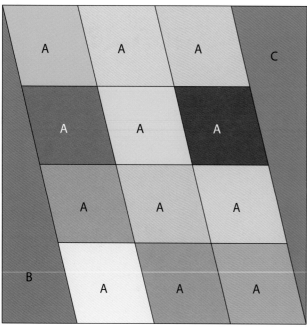

Fabric Requirements and Cutting

Piece	Number to Cut	Size to Cut	Trim Using
A	12	3″ × 3½″	Template A—Pattern 10
B	1	3″ × 10½″	Template B—Pattern 11
C	1	3″ × 10½″	Template C—Pattern 11

All seams are sewn with a ¼″ seam allowance and pressed open.

NOTE

All the pieces in this block are cut using templates from Patterns 10 and 11 (pullout page P1). The dimensions listed in the chart under "Size to Cut" represent the amount of fabric required for each piece. More fabric may be required for shortcut piecing (page 189) or fussy cutting (page 185).

To make a template from a pattern, refer to Making and Using Freezer-Paper Templates (pages 186 and 187). When cutting your fabric, remember to add seam allowances and mark points for matching seams.

Make the Block

1. Arrange and sew the 12 pieces A into 4 rows of 3 each.

2. Sew the 4 rows together to make a larger parallelogram shape that leans to the left. *figure a*

Finish the Block

Sew piece B to the left side of unit A, and piece C to the right side. *figure b*

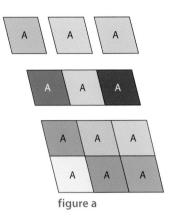

figure a

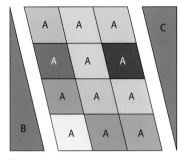

figure b

ALTERNATE IDEAS

Mixed Use

Fabric Requirements and Cutting

Piece	Number to Cut	Size to Cut
A	1	2½″ × 5″
B	1	1½″ × 2½″
C	1	1½″ × 6″
D	1	4″ × 4″
E	1	1½″ × 4″
F	1	1½″ × 5″
G	1	2½″ × 3½″
H	1	3½″ × 5″
I	1	1″ × 3½″
J	1	1″ × 5″
K	1	1″ × 8½″

All seams are sewn with a ¼″ seam allowance and pressed open.

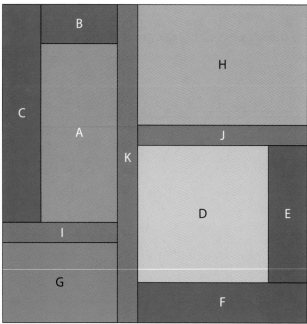

Make the Block

Make the Left Side

1. Sew piece B to the top of piece A.

2. Sew piece C to the left side of unit AB.

3. Sew piece I to the bottom of unit ABC. Sew piece G to the bottom of piece I. *figure a*

Make the Right Side

1. Sew piece E to the right side of piece D.

2. Sew piece F to the bottom of unit DE.

3. Sew piece J to the top of unit DE. Sew piece H to the top of piece J. *figure b*

Finish the Block

Sew the left and right sides together, sewing piece K between them. *figure c*

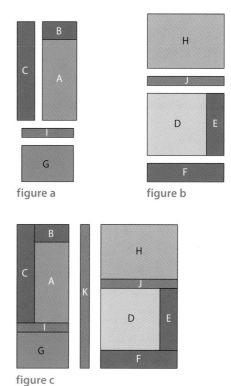

figure a   figure b

figure c

ALTERNATE IDEAS

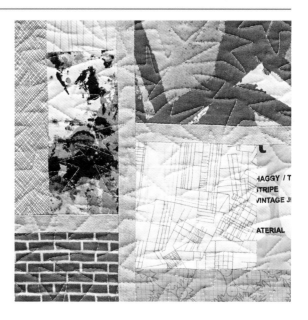

Roadblock

Fabric Requirements and Cutting

Piece	Number to Cut	Size to Cut	Trim Using
A	3	5″ × 6¾″	Template A—Pattern 12
B1	3	3″ × 5¾″	Template B1—Pattern 12
B2	3	3″ × 5¾″	Template B2—Pattern 12
C1	1	2″ × 4″	
C2	1	2″ × 4″	
C3	1	2″ × 3″	
C4	1	2½″ × 3″	
D1	1	3″ × 5¾″	Template D1—Pattern 12
D2	1	3″ × 5¾″	Template D2—Pattern 12

All seams are sewn with a ¼″ seam allowance and pressed open.

NOTE

Some of the pieces in this block are cut using templates from Pattern 12 (pullout page P1). The dimensions listed in the chart under "Size to Cut" represent the amount of fabric required for each piece. More fabric may be required for shortcut piecing (page 189) or fussy cutting (page 185).

To make a template from a pattern, refer to Making and Using Freezer-Paper Templates (pages 186 and 187). When cutting your fabric, remember to add seam allowances and mark points for matching seams.

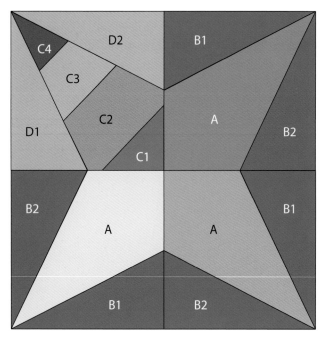

Make the Block

Make the Point Units

1. Sew a piece B1 to a side of a piece A.

2. Sew a piece B2 to the other side of piece A.

3. Repeat Steps 1 and 2 to make a total of
3 point units, each 4½˝ × 4½˝. *figure a*

Make the Contrasting Point Unit

1. Sew together pieces C1, C2, C3, and C4, centering
each piece on the long side of the adjacent piece.

2. Use Template C from Pattern 12 to cut
unit C from the pieced unit. *figure b*

3. Sew piece D1 to a side of pieced unit C.

4. Sew piece D2 to the other side of unit C to
make a point unit 4½˝ × 4½˝. *figure c*

Finish the Block

Arrange and sew the point units in 2 rows of 2 each,
placing the contrasting unit CD in the upper left
corner. Sew the rows together. *figure d*

figure a

figure b

figure c

figure d

ALTERNATE IDEAS

Food Truck

Fabric Requirements and Cutting

Piece	Number to Cut	Size to Cut
A	1	2½″ × 2½″
B	2	1½″ × 3½″
C	2	1½″ × 1½″
D	4	1½″ × 6½″
E	2	1½″ × 6½″
F	2	1½″ × 8½″

All seams are sewn with a ¼″ seam allowance and pressed open.

Make the Block

1. Sew the pieces B together.

2. Sew unit B to the left side of piece A.

3. Sew the pieces C together.

4. Sew unit C to the right side of piece A. *figure a*

5. Sew 3 pieces D together to make unit D. Sew unit D to the bottom of unit ABC. Sew the remaining piece D to the top of unit ABC. *figure b*

Finish the Block

1. Sew pieces E to the top and bottom of the block.

2. Sew pieces F to the left and right sides. *figure c*

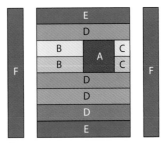

figure a

figure b

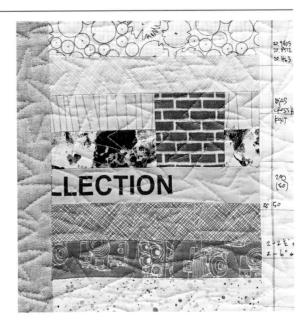

figure c

ALTERNATE IDEAS

Clock Tower

Fabric Requirements and Cutting

Piece	Number to Cut	Size to Cut	Trim Using
A	2	3″ × 10¾″	Template A— Pattern 13
B1	4	2″ × 6¾″	Template B1— Pattern 13
B2	4	2″ × 6¾″	Template B2— Pattern 13
C	1	3″ × 10¾″	Template C— Pattern 13
D1	2	2″ × 6¾″	Template D1— Pattern 13
D2	2	2″ × 6¾″	Template D2— Pattern 13
E	2	1½″ × 8½″	

All seams are sewn with a ¼″ seam allowance and pressed open.

NOTE

All the pieces in this block, except piece E, are cut using templates from Pattern 13 (pullout page P1). The dimensions listed in the chart under "Size to Cut" represent the amount of fabric required for each piece. More fabric may be required for shortcut piecing (page 189) or fussy cutting (page 185).

To make a template from a pattern, refer to Making and Using Freezer-Paper Templates (pages 186 and 187). When cutting your fabric, remember to add seam allowances and mark points for matching seams.

Make the Block

Make the Diamond Units

1. Sew 2 each of pieces B1 and B2 to the 4 sides of a piece A. *figures a & b*

2. Repeat Step 1 to make a second diamond unit.

Make the Contrasting Diamond Unit

Sew 2 each of pieces D1 and D2 to the 4 sides of piece C.

Finish the Block

1. Sew the 3 diamond units together, placing the contrasting diamond in the center.

2. Sew pieces E to the left and right sides of the block. *figure c*

figure a   figure b

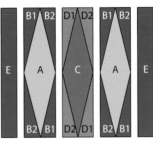

figure c

ALTERNATE IDEAS

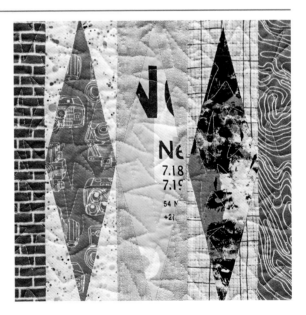

Lobby

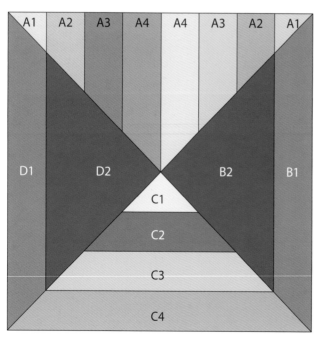

Fabric Requirements and Cutting

Piece	Number to Cut	Size to Cut
A1	2	1½″ × 2″
A2	2	1½″ × 3″
A3	2	1½″ × 4″
A4	2	1½″ × 6″
B1	1	1½″ × 9½″
B2	1	4″ × 7″
C1	1	1½″ × 3″
C2	1	1½″ × 5″
C3	1	1½″ × 7″
C4	1	1½″ × 9½″
D1	1	1½″ × 9½″
D2	1	4″ × 7″

All seams are sewn with a ¼″ seam allowance and pressed open.

NOTE

The large triangles are cut from pieced units using templates from Pattern 14 (pullout page P1). The dimensions listed in the chart under "Size to Cut" represent the amount of fabric required for each piece. More fabric may be required for shortcut piecing (page 189) or fussy cutting (page 185).

To make a template from a pattern, refer to Making and Using Freezer-Paper Templates (pages 186 and 187). When cutting your fabric, remember to add seam allowances around the template and mark points for matching seams.

Make the Block

Make the Triangles

1. For triangle A, sew together pieces A1–A4, aligning the pieces at the top. Use Template A from Pattern 14 to cut triangle A from the pieced unit. *figure a*

2. For triangle B, center and sew piece B2 to piece B1. Use Template B from Pattern 14 to cut triangle B from the pieced unit. *figure b*

3. For triangle C, center and sew together pieces C1–C4. Use Template C from Pattern 14 to cut triangle C from the pieced unit. *figure c*

4. For triangle D, center and sew piece D2 to piece D1. Use Template D from Pattern 14 to cut triangle D from the pieced unit. *figure d*

Finish the Block

1. Sew triangle A to triangle B.

2. Sew triangle C to triangle D.

3. Sew together units AB and CD. *figure e*

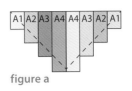

figure a

figure b

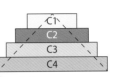

figure c

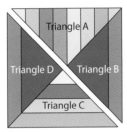

figure d

figure e

ALTERNATE IDEAS

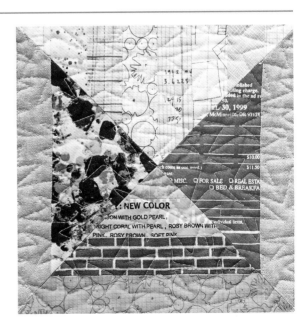

Parking Garage

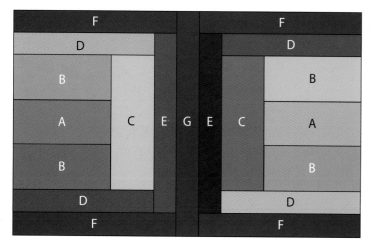

Fabric Requirements and Cutting

Piece	Number to Cut	Size to Cut
A	2	1½″ × 2¾″
B	4	1½″ × 2¾″
C	2	1½″ × 3½″
D	4	1″ × 3¾″
E	2	1″ × 4½″
F	4	1″ × 4¼″
G	1	1″ × 5½″

All seams are sewn with a ¼″ seam allowance and pressed open.

Make the Block

Make the Left Side

1. Sew pieces B to the top and bottom of a piece A.

2. Sew a piece C to the right side of unit AB. *figure a*

3. Sew pieces D to the top and bottom of unit ABC.

4. Sew a piece E to the right side of unit ABCD. *figure b*

Make the Right Side

1. Sew pieces B to the top and bottom of the remaining piece A.

2. Sew piece C to the left side of unit AB. *figure c*

3. Sew pieces D to the top and bottom of unit ABC.

4. Sew piece E to the left side of unit ABCD. *figure d*

Finish the Block

Sew together the left and right sides, sewing piece G between them. *figure e*

figure a   figure b

figure c   figure d

figure e

ALTERNATE IDEAS

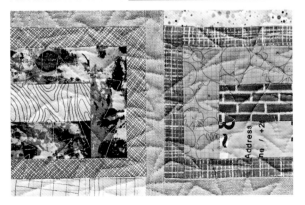

Half Sandwich

Fabric Requirements and Cutting

Piece	Number to Cut	Size to Cut	Trim Using
A1	2	1½″ × 2″	
A2	2	1½″ × 3″	
A3	2	1½″ × 4″	
A4	1	1½″ × 5″	
B	1	6¼″ × 6¼″	Template B—Pattern 18
C	1	4″ × 4″	Template C—Pattern 19
D	1	4″ × 4″	Template D—Pattern 19
E	1	2½″ × 3½″	

All seams are sewn with a ¼″ seam allowance and pressed open.

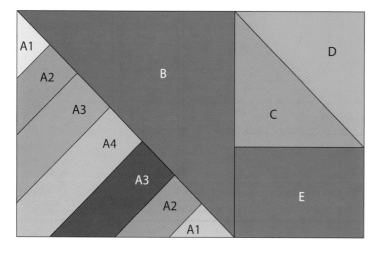

--- **NOTE** ---

Some of the pieces in this block are cut using templates from Patterns 18 and 19 (pullout page P2). The dimensions listed in the chart under "Size to Cut" represent the amount of fabric required for each piece. More fabric may be required for shortcut piecing (page 189) or fussy cutting (page 185).

To make a template from a pattern, refer to Making and Using Freezer-Paper Templates (pages 186 and 187). When cutting your fabric, remember to add seam allowances and mark points for matching seams.

Make the Block

Make the Triangle Units

1. Sew together pieces A1–A4, aligning the pieces at the bottom. Use Template A from Pattern 18 to cut triangle A from the pieced unit. *figure a*

2. Sew together triangle A and piece B to make a square unit 5½″ × 5½″. *figure b*

3. Sew together pieces C and D to make a square unit 3½″ × 3½″. *figure c*

Finish the Block

Sew piece E to the bottom of triangle unit CD. Sew together triangle unit AB and unit CDE. *figure d*

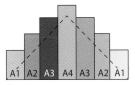

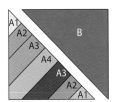

figure a

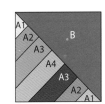

figure b

figure c

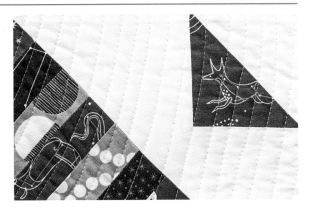

figure d

ALTERNATE IDEAS

Rec Center

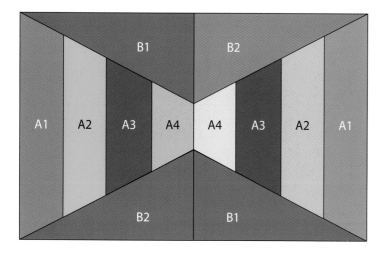

Fabric Requirements and Cutting

Piece	Number to Cut	Size to Cut	Trim Using
A1	2	1½″ × 6″	
A2	2	1½″ × 5″	
A3	2	1½″ × 4″	
A4	2	1½″ × 3″	
B1	2	3″ × 5½″	Template B1—Pattern 20
B2	2	3″ × 5½″	Template B2—Pattern 20

All seams are sewn with a ¼″ seam allowance and pressed open.

NOTE

Some of the pieces in this block are cut using templates from Pattern 20 (pullout page P2). The dimensions listed in the chart under "Size to Cut" represent the amount of fabric required for each piece. More fabric may be required for shortcut piecing (page 189) or fussy cutting (page 185).

To make a template from a pattern, refer to Making and Using Freezer-Paper Templates (pages 186 and 187). When cutting your fabric, remember to add seam allowances and mark points for matching seams.

Make the Block

Make the Left Side

1. Center and sew together pieces A1–A4. Use Template A from Pattern 20 to cut unit A from the pieced unit. *figure a*

2. Sew pieces B1 and B2 to unit A to make a pieced unit 4½″ × 5½″. *figure b*

Make the Right Side

1. Center and sew together pieces A4–A1. Use Template A from Pattern 20 to cut unit A from the pieced unit. *figure c*

2. Sew pieces B2 and B1 to unit A to make a pieced unit 4½″ × 5½″. *figure d*

Finish the Block

Sew together the left and right sides. *figure e*

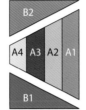

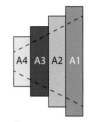

figure a   figure b   figure c

figure d   figure e

ALTERNATE IDEAS

Onramp

Fabric Requirements and Cutting

Piece	Number to Cut	Size to Cut	Trim Using
A1	2	1½″ × 3¾″	
A2	2	1½″ × 4¼″	
A3	3	1½″ × 2″	
A4	3	1½″ × 2½″	
A5	1	1½″ × 5″	
B	1	1½″ × 3½″	
C	1	3½″ × 9″	Template C—Pattern 21

All seams are sewn with a ¼″ seam allowance and pressed open.

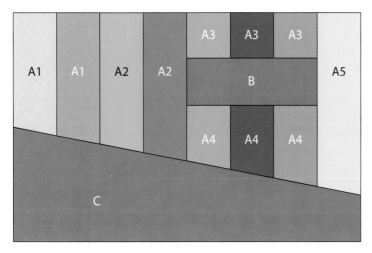

---------------- **NOTE** ----------------

Most of the pieces in this block are cut using templates from Pattern 21 (pullout page P2). The dimensions listed in the chart under "Size to Cut" represent the amount of fabric required for each piece. More fabric may be required for shortcut piecing (page 189) or fussy cutting (page 185).

To make a template from a pattern, refer to Making and Using Freezer-Paper Templates (pages 186 and 187). When cutting your fabric, remember to add seam allowances and mark points for matching seams.

Make the Block

1. Sew together pieces A3.

2. Sew together pieces A4.

3. Sew unit A3 and unit A4 to piece B. *figure a*

4. Sew piece A5 to unit AB, aligning the top edges. *figure b*

5. Sew together 2 pieces A1 and 2 pieces A2, aligning the top edges. *figure c*

6. Sew the pieced unit from Step 5 to the unit from Step 4, aligning the top edges. Use Template A from Pattern 21 to cut unit A from the pieced unit. *figure d*

7. Sew piece C to the bottom of the block. *figure e*

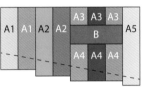

figure a

figure b

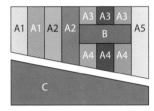

figure c

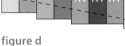

figure d

figure e

ALTERNATE IDEAS

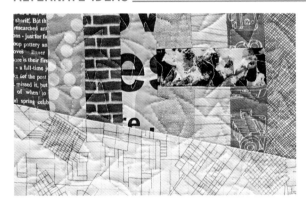

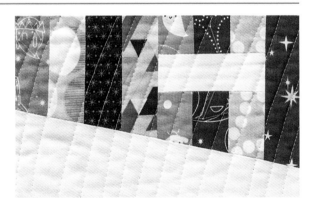

Planter Box

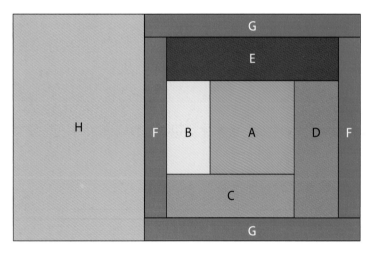

Fabric Requirements and Cutting

Piece	Number to Cut	Size to Cut
A	1	2½″ × 2½″
B	1	1½″ × 2½″
C	1	1½″ × 3½″
D	1	1½″ × 3½″
E	1	1½″ × 4½″
F	2	1″ × 4½″
G	2	1″ × 5½″
H	1	3½″ × 5½″

All seams are sewn with a ¼″ seam allowance and pressed open.

Make the Block

1. Sew piece B to the left side of piece A.

2. Sew piece C to the bottom.

3. Sew piece D to the right side.

4. Sew piece E to the top. *figure a*

5. Sew pieces F to both sides.

6. Sew pieces G to the top and bottom. *figure b*

7. Sew piece H to the left side. *figure c*

figure a

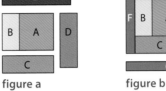

figure b

figure c

ALTERNATE IDEAS

Sequins

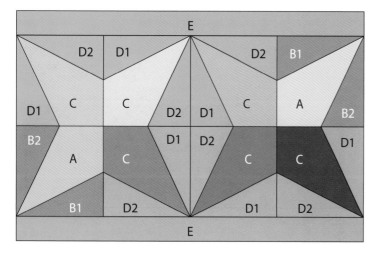

Fabric Requirements and Cutting

Piece	Number to Cut	Size to Cut	Trim Using
A	2	2½″ × 4¼″	Template A—Pattern 22
B1	2	2″ × 3½″	Template B1—Pattern 22
B2	2	2″ × 3½″	Template B2—Pattern 22
C	6	2½″ × 4¼″	Template C—Pattern 22
D1	6	2″ × 3½″	Template D1—Pattern 22
D2	6	2″ × 3½″	Template D2—Pattern 22
E	2	1″ × 8½″	

All seams are sewn with a ¼″ seam allowance and pressed open.

NOTE

Most of the pieces in this block are cut using templates from Pattern 22 (pullout page P1). The dimensions listed in the chart under "Size to Cut" represent the amount of fabric required for each piece. More fabric may be required for shortcut piecing (page 189) or fussy cutting (page 185).

To make a template from a pattern, refer to Making and Using Freezer-Paper Templates (pages 186 and 187). When cutting your fabric, remember to add seam allowances and mark points for matching seams.

Make the Block

Make the Contrasting Point Units

Sew pieces B1 and B2 to a piece A. Repeat to make a total of 2 contrasting point units, each 2½" × 2½". *figure a*

figure a

figure b

Make the Point Units

Sew 1 each of pieces D1 and D2 to a piece C. Repeat to make a total of 6 point units, each 2½" × 2½". *figure b*

figure c

figure d

Make Two Stars

1. Sew 3 point units and a contrasting point unit into 2 rows of 2 units each. For the left star, place the contrasting unit in the lower left corner.

2. Sew the rows together. *figure c*

3. Repeat Steps 1 and 2, placing the contrasting unit in the upper right corner, to make the right star. *figure d*

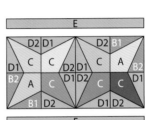

figure e

Finish the Block

1. Sew together the left and right stars.

2. Sew pieces E to the top and bottom of the block. *figure e*

ALTERNATE IDEAS

Emergency Exit

Fabric Requirements and Cutting

Piece	Number to Cut	Size to Cut
A	3	1½″ × 3½″
B	4	1″ × 3½″
C	2	1½″ × 5½″
D	1	1½″ × 5½″
E	1	2½″ × 5½″

All seams are sewn with a ¼″ seam allowance and pressed open.

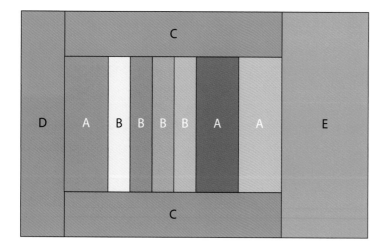

Make the Block

1. Sew together pieces A and B. *figure a*

2. Sew pieces C to the top and bottom of unit AB.

3. Sew piece D to the left side of the block.

4. Sew piece E to the right side of the block. *figure b*

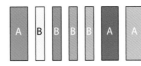

figure a

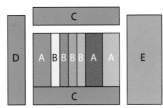

figure b

ALTERNATE IDEAS

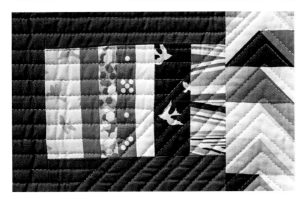

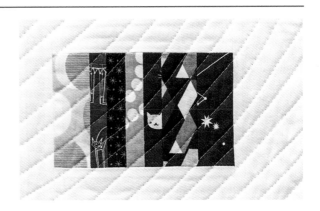

House Plant

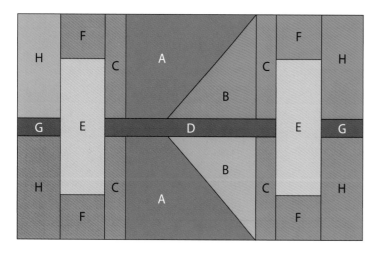

Fabric Requirements and Cutting

Piece	Number to Cut	Size to Cut
A	2	2¾″ × 3½″
B	2	2¼″ × 2¼″
C	4	1″ × 2¾″
D	1	1″ × 4½″
E	2	1½″ × 3½″
F	4	1½″ × 1½″
G	2	1″ × 1½″
H	4	1½″ × 2¾″

All seams are sewn with a ¼″ seam allowance and pressed open.

SEWING DIAGONAL SEAMS

Align the 2 pieces of fabric with right sides together. Use a fabric marker to draw the diagonal seam line as shown in the diagram. Sew along the marked line. Trim away the excess fabric to leave a ¼″ seam allowance. Press the seam open.

Make the Block

Make the Center Unit

For Steps 1 and 2, refer to Sewing Diagonal Seams (page 74).

1. Place a piece B on top of a piece A. Mark and sew the diagonal seam. *figure a*

2. Place the remaining piece B on top of the remaining piece A. Mark and sew the diagonal seam. *figure b*

3. Sew 2 pieces C to each unit AB.

4. Sew piece D between the 2 pieced units ABC. *figure c*

Make the Side Units

1. Sew 2 pieces F to each piece E. *figure d*

2. Sew 2 pieces H to each piece G. *figure e*

3. Sew a unit EF to the right side of a unit GH. This is the left-side unit. *figure f*

4. Sew a unit EF to the left side of a unit GH. This is the right-side unit. *figure g*

Finish the Block

Sew the left and right side units to the center unit. *figure h*

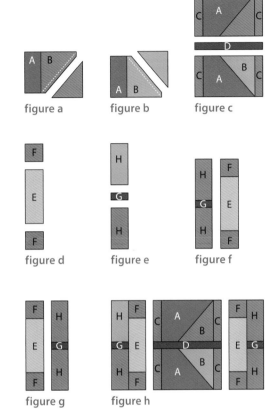

figure a figure b figure c

figure d figure e figure f

figure g figure h

ALTERNATE IDEAS

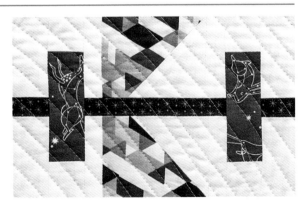

Waterfront

Fabric Requirements and Cutting

Piece	Number to Cut	Size to Cut
A	3	1½″ × 3½″
B	6	1½″ × 1½″
C	2	1½″ × 2″
D	4	2″ × 2½″
E	2	1½″ × 1½″
F	4	1½″ × 2½″

All seams are sewn with a ¼″ seam allowance and pressed open.

Make the Block

1. Sew 2 pieces B to each piece A to create 3 units AB. *figure a*

2. Sew 2 pieces D to each piece C to create 2 units CD. *figure b*

3. Sew 2 pieces F to each piece E to create 2 units EF. *figure c*

4. Sew together the pieced units. *figure d*

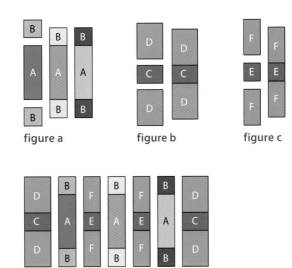

figure a   figure b   figure c

figure d

ALTERNATE IDEAS

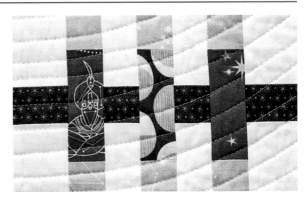

Meow

Fabric Requirements and Cutting

Piece	Number to Cut	Size to Cut
A	6	1½″ × 3½″
B	2	2½″ × 2½″
C	3	2½″ × 2½″
D	2	1½″ × 5½″

All seams are sewn with a ¼″ seam allowance and pressed open.

───── **SEWING DIAGONAL SEAMS** ─────

Align the 2 pieces of fabric with right sides together. Use a fabric marker to draw the diagonal seam line as shown in the diagram. Sew along the marked line. Trim away the excess fabric to leave a ¼″ seam allowance. Press the seam open.

Make the Block

For Steps 2 and 3, refer to Sewing Diagonal Seams (page 78).

1. Sew together 2 pieces A. Repeat to make 3 units A. *figure a*

2. Place a piece B on top of a unit A. Mark and sew the diagonal seam. *figure b*

3. Place the remaining piece B on top of a unit A. Mark and sew the diagonal seam. Note that this seam is the mirror image of the one in Step 2. *figure c*

4. Sew together the 2 units AB and the remaining unit A. *figure d*

5. Sew together pieces C. Sew unit C to the bottom of unit AB. *figure e*

6. Sew pieces D to the sides of the block. *figure f*

figure a   figure b   figure c

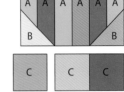

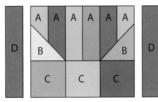

figure d   figure e

figure f

ALTERNATE IDEAS

Magazine Rack

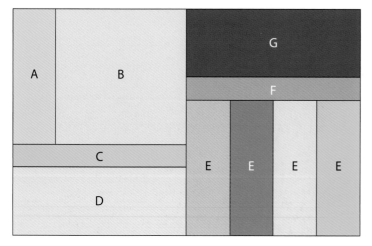

Fabric Requirements and Cutting

Piece	Number to Cut	Size to Cut
A	1	1½″ × 3½″
B	1	3½″ × 3½″
C	1	1″ × 4½″
D	1	2″ × 4½″
E	4	1½″ × 3½″
F	1	1½″ × 4½″
G	1	2″ × 4½″

All seams are sewn with a ¼″ seam allowance and pressed open.

Make the Block

Make the Left Side

1. Sew together pieces A and B.

2. Sew piece C to the bottom of unit AB.

3. Sew piece D to the bottom of unit ABC. *figure a*

Make the Right Side

1. Sew pieces E together.

2. Sew piece F to the top of unit E.

3. Sew piece G to the top of unit EF. *figure b*

Finish the Block

Sew together the left and right sides. *figure c*

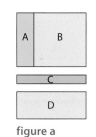

figure a

figure b

figure c

ALTERNATE IDEAS

Kiosk

Fabric Requirements and Cutting

Piece	Number to Cut	Size to Cut	Trim Using
A	1	4″ × 6½″	Template A— Pattern 23
B1	1	3¾″ × 4¼″	Template B1— Pattern 23
B2	1	3¾″ × 4¼″	Template B2— Pattern 23
C	1	3½″ × 3½″	
D	2	1½″ × 3½″	
E	2	1½″ × 5½″	

All seams are sewn with a ¼″ seam allowance and pressed open.

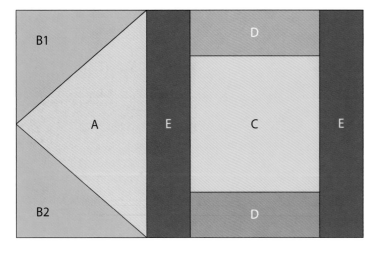

NOTE

Some of the pieces in this block are cut using templates from Pattern 23 (pullout page P1). The dimensions listed in the chart under "Size to Cut" represent the amount of fabric required for each piece. More fabric may be required for shortcut piecing (page 189) or fussy cutting (page 185).

To make a template from a pattern, refer to Making and Using Freezer-Paper Templates (pages 186 and 187). When cutting your fabric, remember to add seam allowances and mark points for matching seams.

Make the Block

1. Sew pieces B1 and B2 to piece A to make the unit AB, 3½″ × 5½″. *figure a*

2. Sew pieces D to the top and bottom of piece C. *figure b*

3. Sew pieces E to the left and right sides of unit CD. *figure c*

4. Sew unit AB to the left side of unit CDE. *figure d*

figure a

figure b

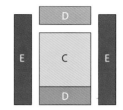
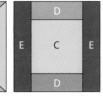
figure c

figure d

ALTERNATE IDEAS

Parking Meters

Fabric Requirements and Cutting

Piece	Number to Cut	Size to Cut
A	1	2½″ × 4½″
B	1	1½″ × 4½″
C	1	1½″ × 3½″
D	1	1½″ × 2½″
E	1	2½″ × 3½″
F	1	1½″ × 2½″
G	3	1½″ × 5½″

All seams are sewn with a ¼″ seam allowance and pressed open.

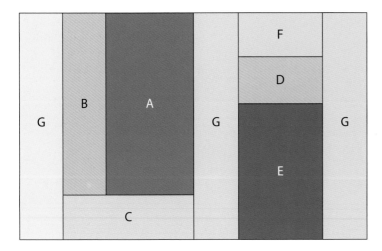

Make the Block

1. Sew together pieces A and B.

2. Sew piece C to the bottom of unit AB. *figure a*

3. Sew together pieces D and E.

4. Sew piece F to the top of unit DE. *figure b*

5. Sew together the pieced units and the 3 pieces G. *figure c*

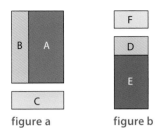

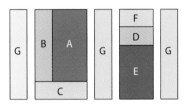

figure a   figure b

figure c

ALTERNATE IDEAS

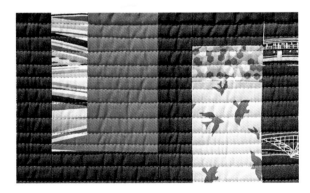

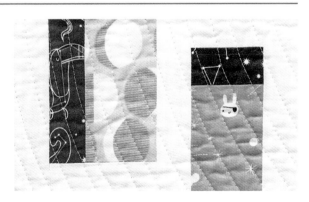

Turnstile

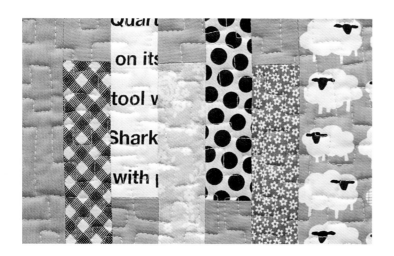

Fabric Requirements and Cutting

Piece	Number to Cut	Size to Cut
A	5	1½″ × 4½″
B	5	1½″ × 1½″
C	1	1½″ × 5½″
D	1	2½″ × 5½″

All seams are sewn with a ¼″ seam allowance and pressed open.

Make the Block

1. Arrange the 5 pieces A in a row. Sew pieces B to the tops of the first, third, and fifth pieces A. Sew pieces B to the bottoms of the second and fourth pieces A. *figure a*

2. Sew together the units AB.

Finish the Block

1. Sew piece C to the left side of unit AB.

2. Sew piece D to the right side of unit ABC. *figure b*

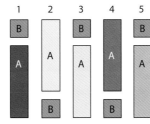

figure a

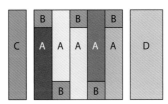

figure b

ALTERNATE IDEAS

Rose Garden

Fabric Requirements and Cutting

Piece	Number to Cut	Size to Cut
A	1	2½″ × 2½″
B	2	2″ × 2½″
C	2	1″ × 2½″
D	4	1″ × 2″
E	4	1″ × 3½″
F	2	1½″ × 3½″
G	4	1½″ × 2½″
H	4	1″ × 2¾″
I	2	1″ × 1″

All seams are sewn with a ¼″ seam allowance and pressed open.

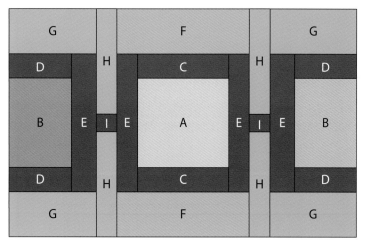

Make the Block

Make the Center

1. Sew pieces C to piece A.

2. Sew pieces E to unit AC.

3. Sew pieces F to unit ACE. *figure a*

Make the Sides

1. Sew 2 pieces D to each piece B.

2. Sew a piece E to the right side of a unit BD.

3. Sew a piece E to the left side of the other unit BD.

4. Sew 2 pieces G to each unit BDE. *figures b & c*

Finish the Block

1. Sew pieces H to each piece I. *figure d*

2. Sew together the pieced units, noting the orientation of the side units. *figure e*

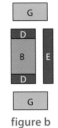
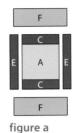

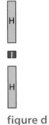

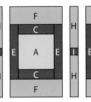
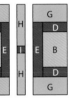

figure a   figure b   figure c

figure d   figure e

ALTERNATE IDEAS

Supermarket

Fabric Requirements and Cutting

Piece	Number to Cut	Size to Cut	Trim Using
A	3	3″ × 6½″	Template A—Pattern 24
B1	6	2″ × 4¼″	Template B1—Pattern 24
B2	6	2″ × 4¼″	Template B2—Pattern 24
C	1	3″ × 6½″	Template C—Pattern 24
D1	2	2″ × 4¼″	Template D1—Pattern 24
D2	2	2″ × 4¼″	Template D2—Pattern 24

All seams are sewn with a ¼″ seam allowance and pressed open.

NOTE

All the pieces in this block are cut using templates from Pattern 24 (pullout page P1). The dimensions listed in the chart under "Size to Cut" represent the amount of fabric required for each piece. More fabric may be required for shortcut piecing (page 189) or fussy cutting (page 185).

To make a template from a pattern, refer to Making and Using Freezer-Paper Templates (pages 186 and 187). When cutting your fabric, remember to add seam allowances and mark points for matching seams.

Make the Block

Make the Diamond Units

1. Sew pieces B1 to opposite sides of a piece A.

2. Sew pieces B2 to the remaining sides of piece A to make a diamond unit, 2½″ × 5½″.

3. Repeat Steps 1 and 2 to create a total of 3 diamond units. *figures a & b*

Make the Contrasting Diamond Unit

1. Sew pieces D1 to opposite sides of piece C.

2. Sew pieces D2 to the remaining sides of piece C to make a contrasting diamond unit, 2½″ × 5½″. *figure c*

Finish the Block

Sew together the diamond units, placing the contrasting unit third from the left. *figure d*

figure a

figure b

figure c

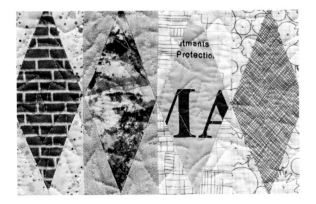
figure d

ALTERNATE IDEAS

Bowling Alley

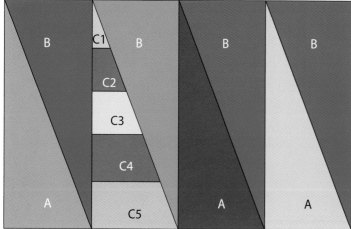

Fabric Requirements and Cutting

Piece	Number to Cut	Size to Cut	Trim Using
A	3	3″ × 7″	Template A/C—Pattern 25
B	4	3″ × 7″	Template B—Pattern 25
C1	1	1½″ × 1½″	
C2	1	1½″ × 1¾″	
C3	1	1½″ × 2¼″	
C4	1	1½″ × 2½″	
C5	1	1½″ × 3″	

All seams are sewn with a ¼″ seam allowance and pressed open.

─── **NOTE** ───

Some of the pieces in this block are cut using templates from Pattern 25 (pullout page P1). The dimensions listed in the chart under "Size to Cut" represent the amount of fabric required for each piece. More fabric may be required for shortcut piecing (page 189) or fussy cutting (page 185).

To make a template from a pattern, refer to Making and Using Freezer-Paper Templates (pages 186 and 187). When cutting your fabric, remember to add seam allowances and mark points for matching seams.

Make the Block

Make the Triangle Units

Sew together a piece A and a piece B to make a triangle unit, 2½" × 5½". Repeat to make a total of 3 triangle units. *figure a*

Make the Contrasting Triangle Unit

1. Sew together pieces C1–C5, aligning the short sides at the left. Use Template C from Pattern 25 to cut triangle C from the pieced unit. *figure b*

2. Sew together triangle C and the remaining piece B to make the contrasting triangle unit, 2½" × 5½". *figure c*

Finish the Block

Sew together the triangle units. *figure d*

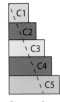

figure a   figure b   figure c

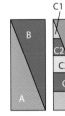

figure d

ALTERNATE IDEAS

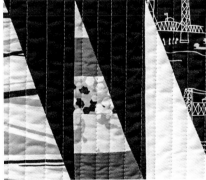

Karaoke

Fabric Requirements and Cutting

Piece	Number to Cut	Size to Cut
A	1	2½˝ × 2½˝
B	1	1½˝ × 2½˝
C	1	2½˝ × 2½˝
D	1	1½˝ × 5½˝
E	1	2½˝ × 5½˝
F	15	1½˝ × 1½˝

All seams are sewn with a ¼˝ seam allowance and pressed open.

Make the Block

Make the Left Side

1. Sew piece B to the top of piece A.

2. Sew piece C to the bottom of unit AB.

3. Sew piece D to the left side of unit ABC.

4. Sew piece E to the right side of unit ABCD.
figure a

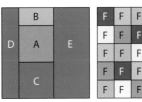

figure a

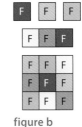

figure b

Make the Right Side

1. Arrange and sew the F pieces in 5 rows of 3 each.

2. Sew together the 5 rows. *figure b*

Finish the Block

Sew together the left and right sides. *figure c*

figure c

ALTERNATE IDEAS

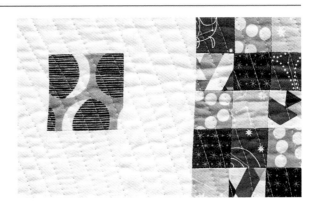

Traffic Cones

Fabric Requirements and Cutting

Piece	Number to Cut	Size to Cut	Trim Using
A1	1	2½″ × 3″	
A2	1	2½″ × 5″	
B	3	3″ × 7″	Template B—Pattern 26
C	5	3″ × 7″	Template C—Pattern 26

All seams are sewn with a ¼″ seam allowance and pressed open.

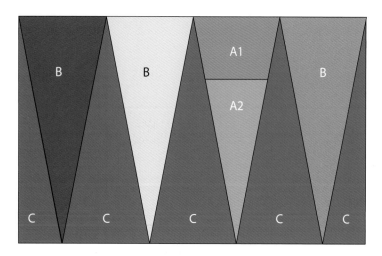

NOTE

Some of the pieces in this block are cut using templates from Pattern 26 (pullout page P2). The dimensions listed in the chart under "Size to Cut" represent the amount of fabric required for each piece. More fabric may be required for shortcut piecing (page 189) or fussy cutting (page 185).

To make a template from a pattern, refer to Making and Using Freezer-Paper Templates (pages 186 and 187). When cutting your fabric, remember to add seam allowances and mark points for matching seams.

Make the Block

1. Sew together pieces A1 and A2.

2. Use Template A from Pattern 26 to cut unit A from the pieced unit. *figure a*

3. Sew together unit A and pieces B and C. *figure b*

Finish the Block

Trim the excess fabric from the sides to make a block 5½″ × 8½″. *figure c*

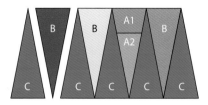

figure a   figure b

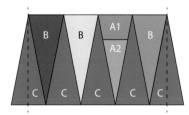

figure c

ALTERNATE IDEAS

Raindrops

Fabric Requirements and Cutting

Piece	Number to Cut	Size to Cut
A	4	2½″ × 2½″
B	1	2½″ × 3½″
C	2	1½″ × 2½″
D	1	1½″ × 2½″
E	2	1½″ × 3½″
F	2	1½″ × 1½″
G	1	2½″ × 2½″

All seams are sewn with a ¼″ seam allowance and pressed open.

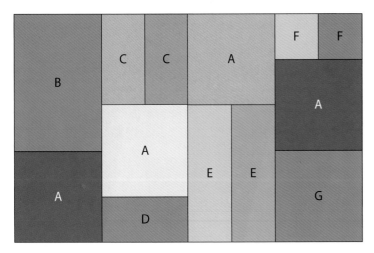

Make the Block

Make Column 1

Sew a piece A to the bottom of piece B. *figure a*

Make Column 2

1. Sew together pieces C.

2. Sew a piece A to the bottom of unit C.

3. Sew piece D to the bottom of piece A. *figure b*

Make Column 3

1. Sew together pieces E.

2. Sew a piece A to the top of unit E. *figure c*

Make Column 4

1. Sew together pieces F.

2. Sew the remaining piece A to the bottom of unit F.

3. Sew piece G to the bottom of piece A. *figure d*

Finish the Block

Sew the 4 columns together. *figure e*

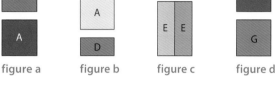

figure a   figure b   figure c   figure d

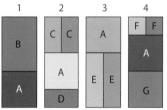

figure e

ALTERNATE IDEAS

Stripey Socks

Fabric Requirements and Cutting

Piece	Number to Cut	Size to Cut
A	2	2½″ × 8″
B	2	1¼″ × 8″
C	2	1¼″ × 8″
D	2	1¼″ × 8″
E	2	1¼″ × 8″
F	2	2½″ × 8″

All seams are sewn with a ¼″ seam allowance and pressed open.

NOTE

Each stripe requires 2 pieces of fabric. If you want the look of continuous stripes, use 2 pieces of the same fabric for each lettered piece.

Make the Block

Make Columns 1 and 3

1. Sew together pieces A–F, aligning each piece ½"
to the left of the piece above it.

2. Use the 60° markings on your ruler to cut
2 pieced strips, each 2½" wide. These are
columns 1 and 3. *figure a*

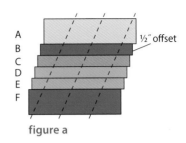

figure a

Make Columns 2 and 4

1. Sew together pieces A–F, aligning each piece ½"
to the right of the piece above it.

2. Use the 60° markings on your ruler to cut
2 pieced strips, each 2½" wide. These are
columns 2 and 4. *figure b*

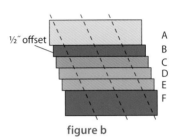

figure b

Finish the Block

1. Sew together the columns, matching the seams
between the stripes.

2. Trim away the excess fabric to make a block
5½" × 8½". *figure c*

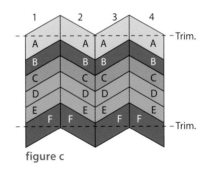

figure c

ALTERNATE IDEAS

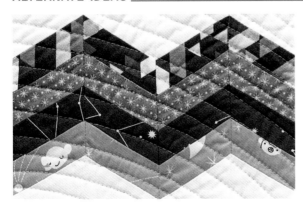

Sidewalk

Fabric Requirements and Cutting

Piece	Number to Cut	Size to Cut
A	9	1½″ × 1½″
B	2	1½″ × 3½″
C	1	1½″ × 5½″
D	1	3½″ × 3½″
E	1	1½″ × 3½″
F	2	1½″ × 4½″

All seams are sewn with a ¼″ seam allowance and pressed open.

Make the Block

Make the Left Side

1. Arrange and sew the pieces A in 3 rows of 3 each.

2. Sew the rows together to make a 9-patch unit. *figure a*

3. Sew pieces B to the top and bottom of unit A.

4. Sew piece C to the left side of unit AB. *figure b*

Make the Right Side

1. Sew piece E to the right side of piece D.

2. Sew pieces F to the top and bottom of unit DE. *figure c*

Finish the Block

Sew together the left and right sides. *figure d*

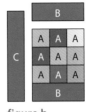
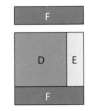

figure a

figure b

figure c

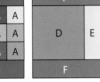

figure d

ALTERNATE IDEAS

Fortune Cookies

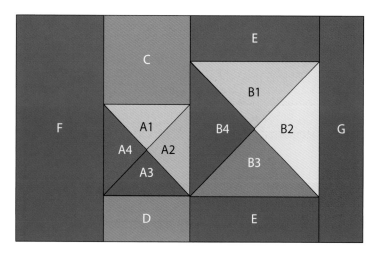

Fabric Requirements and Cutting

Piece	Number to Cut	Size to Cut	Trim Using
A1	1	2″ × 3¾″	Template A1— Pattern 27
A2	1	2″ × 3¾″	Template A2— Pattern 27
A3	1	2″ × 3¾″	Template A3— Pattern 27
A4	1	2″ × 3¾″	Template A4— Pattern 27
B1	1	2½″ × 4¾″	Template B1— Pattern 28
B2	1	2½″ × 4¾″	Template B2— Pattern 28
B3	1	2½″ × 4¾″	Template B3— Pattern 28
B4	1	2½″ × 4¾″	Template B4— Pattern 28
C	1	2½″ × 2½″	
D	1	1½″ × 2½″	
E	2	1½″ × 3½″	
F	1	2½″ × 5½″	
G	1	1½″ × 5½″	

All seams are sewn with a ¼″ seam allowance and pressed open.

NOTE

Most of the pieces in this block are cut using templates from Patterns 27 and 28 (pullout page P2). The dimensions listed in the chart under "Size to Cut" represent the amount of fabric required for each piece. More fabric may be required for shortcut piecing (page 189) or fussy cutting (page 185).

To make a template from a pattern, refer to Making and Using Freezer-Paper Templates (pages 186 and 187). When cutting your fabric, remember to add seam allowances and mark points for matching seams.

Make the Block

Make the Small Cookie Unit

1. Sew together pieces A1 and A2.

2. Sew together pieces A3 and A4.

3. Sew together units A1A2 and A3A4 to create a square 2½″ × 2½″. *figure a*

4. Sew piece C to the top of unit A, and piece D to the bottom. *figure b*

Make the Large Cookie Unit

1. Sew together pieces B1 and B2.

2. Sew together pieces B3 and B4.

3. Sew together units B1B2 and B3B4 to create a square 3½″ × 3½″. *figure c*

4. Sew pieces E to the top and bottom of unit B. *figure d*

Finish the Block

1. Sew together the small and large cookie units.

2. Sew piece F to the left side and piece G to the right side. *figure e*

figure a

figure b

figure c

figure d

figure e

ALTERNATE IDEAS

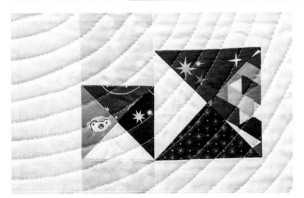

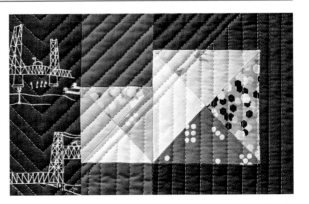

Airport

Fabric Requirements and Cutting

Piece	Number to Cut	Size to Cut
A	8	1¼″ × 10½″
B	1	5″ × 5″

All seams are sewn with a ¼″ seam allowance and pressed open.

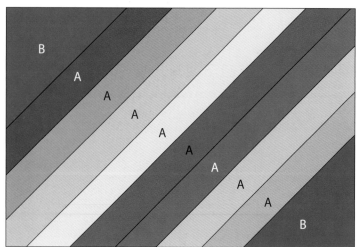

Make the Block

1. Sew together pieces A. The completed unit will measure 8½″ × 10½″. *figure a*

2. Cut piece B in half diagonally from corner to corner. *figure b*

3. Position the long edge of a triangle piece B 1½″ down from the top right corner of unit A. Sew together.

4. Position the long edge of the other triangle piece B piece 1½″ up from the bottom left corner of unit A. Sew together. *figure c*

5. Trim away the excess fabric to create a block 5½″ × 8½″. *figure d*

———————— **NOTE** ————————

If desired, cut a piece of regular or freezer paper 5½″ × 8½″ to use as a guide for cutting the finished block.

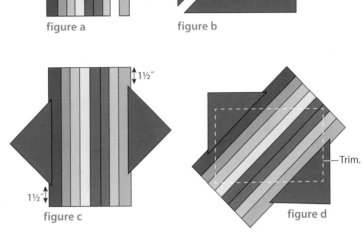

figure a   figure b

figure c   figure d

ALTERNATE IDEAS

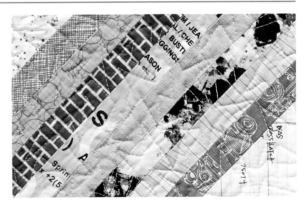

Skyline

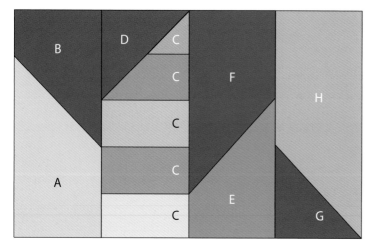

Fabric Requirements and Cutting

Piece	Number to Cut	Size to Cut
A	1	2½″ × 4½″
B	1	2½″ × 3½″
C	5	1½″ × 2½″
D	1	2½″ × 2½″
E	1	2½″ × 3½″
F	1	2½″ × 4½″
G	1	2½″ × 2½″
H	1	2½″ × 5½″

All seams are sewn with a ¼″ seam allowance and pressed open.

—— SEWING DIAGONAL SEAMS ——

Align the 2 pieces of fabric with right sides together. Use a fabric marker to draw the diagonal seam line as shown in the diagram. Sew along the marked line. Trim away the excess fabric to leave a ¼″ seam allowance. Press the seam open.

Make the Block

For all columns, refer to Sewing Diagonal Seams (page 108).

Make Column 1

Place piece B on top of piece A. Mark and sew the diagonal seam. *figure a*

figure a

figure b

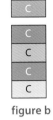
figure c

Make Column 2

1. Sew together the pieces C. *figure b*

2. Place piece D on top of unit C. Mark and sew the diagonal seam. *figure c*

Make Column 3

Place piece F on top of piece E. Mark and sew the diagonal seam. *figure d*

figure d

figure e

Make Column 4

Place piece G on top of piece H. Mark and sew the diagonal seam. *figure e*

Finish the Block

Sew the columns together. *figure f*

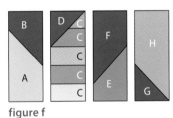
figure f

ALTERNATE IDEAS

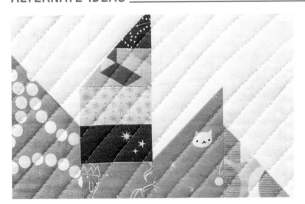

City Hall

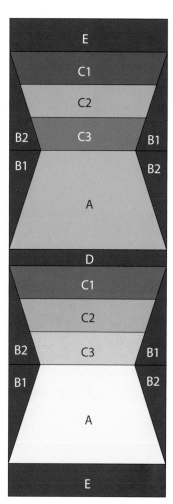

Fabric Requirements and Cutting

Piece	Number to Cut	Size to Cut	Trim Using
A	2	4″ × 6″	Template A— Pattern 29
B1	4	2″ × 5½″	Template B1— Pattern 29
B2	4	2″ × 5½″	Template B2— Pattern 29
C1	2	1½″ × 6″	
C2	2	1½″ × 5½″	
C3	2	1½″ × 4¾″	
D	1	1″ × 5½″	
E	2	1¼″ × 5½″	

All seams are sewn with a ¼″ seam allowance and pressed open.

------ **NOTE** ------

Some of the pieces in this block will be cut using templates from Pattern 29 (pullout page P2). The dimensions listed in the chart under "Size to Cut" represent the amount of fabric required for each piece. More fabric may be required for shortcut piecing (page 189) or fussy cutting (page 185).

To make a template from a pattern, refer to Making and Using Freezer-Paper Templates (pages 186 and 187). When cutting your fabric, remember to add seam allowances and mark points for matching seams.

Make the Block

1. Sew one each of pieces B1 and B2 to a piece A. Repeat to create 2 units AB, each 3½″ × 5½″. *figure a*

2. Sew together pieces C1, C2, and C3 so that each piece is centered below the adjacent piece.

3. Use Template C from Pattern 29 to cut unit C from the pieced unit. *figure b*

4. Sew pieces B2 and B1 to unit C. Repeat to create 2 units BC, each 3½″ × 5½″. *figure c*

Finish the Block

1. Sew together a unit AB and a unit BC to make an hourglass shape 5½″ × 6½″. Repeat to make a second unit AB/BC. *figure d*

2. Sew piece D between the 2 ABC units.

3. Sew pieces E to the top and bottom of the block. *figure e*

figure a

figure b

figure c

figure d

figure e

ALTERNATE IDEAS

Zoo Train

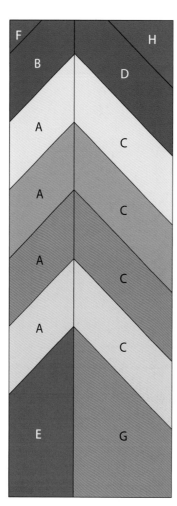

Fabric Requirements and Cutting

Piece	Number to Cut	Size to Cut	Trim Using
A	4	2¼″ × 6″	Template A—Pattern 30
B	1	3″ × 4½″	Template B—Pattern 30
C	4	2½″ × 6¾″	Template C—Pattern 30
D	1	4″ × 5½″	Template D—Pattern 30
E	1	3″ × 6¼″	Template E—Pattern 30
F	1	1½″ × 1½″	
G	1	4″ × 6¼″	Template G—Pattern 30
H	1	2½″ × 2½″	

All seams are sewn with a ¼″ seam allowance and pressed open.

─────────── **NOTE** ───────────

Most of the pieces in this block are cut using templates from Pattern 30 (pullout page P2). The dimensions listed in the chart under "Size to Cut" represent the amount of fabric required for each piece. More fabric may be required for shortcut piecing (page 189) or fussy cutting (page 185).

To make a template from a pattern, refer to Making and Using Freezer-Paper Templates (pages 186 and 187). When cutting your fabric, remember to add seam allowances and mark points for matching seams.

────── **SEWING DIAGONAL SEAMS** ──────

Align the 2 pieces of fabric with right sides together. Use a fabric marker to draw the diagonal seam line as shown in the diagram. Sew along the marked line. Trim away the excess fabric to leave a ¼″ seam allowance. Press the seam open.

Make the Block

For each Step 2 below, refer to Sewing Diagonal Seams (page 112).

Make the Left Side

1. Sew together pieces A. Sew piece B to the top of unit A, and sew piece E to the bottom. *figure a*

2. Place piece F on top of unit ABE. Mark and sew the diagonal seam. *figure b*

Make the Right Side

1. Sew together pieces C. Sew piece D to the top of unit C, and sew piece G to the bottom. *figure c*

2. Place piece H on top of unit CDG. Mark and sew the diagonal seam. *figure d*

Finish the Block

Sew together the left and right sides. *figure e*

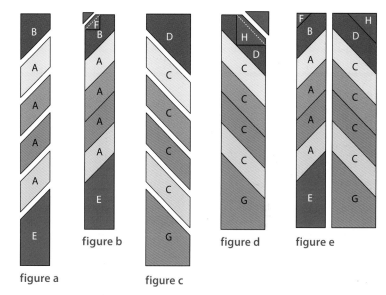

figure a

figure b

figure c

figure d

figure e

ALTERNATE IDEAS _____

Brewery

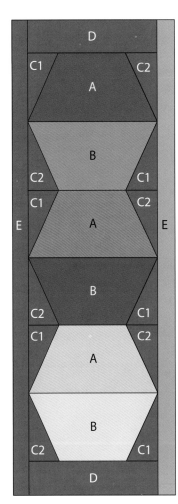

Fabric Requirements and Cutting

Piece	Number to Cut	Size to Cut	Trim Using
A	3	3″ × 5¼″	Template A—Pattern 31
B	3	3″ × 5¼″	Template B—Pattern 31
C1	6	2″ × 3″	Template C1—Pattern 31
C2	6	2″ × 3″	Template C2—Pattern 31
D	2	1½″ × 4½″	
E	2	1″ × 14½″	

All seams are sewn with a ¼″ seam allowance and pressed open.

NOTE

Most of the pieces in this block are cut using templates from Pattern 31 (pullout page P1). The dimensions listed in the chart under "Size to Cut" represent the amount of fabric required for each piece. More fabric may be required for shortcut piecing (page 189) or fussy cutting (page 185).

To make a template from a pattern, refer to Making and Using Freezer-Paper Templates (pages 186 and 187). When cutting your fabric, remember to add seam allowances and mark points for matching seams.

Make the Block

1. Sew a piece C1 to the left side of each piece A, and a piece C2 to the right side, to make a unit AC, 2½″ × 4½″. Repeat to make a total of 3 units AC. *figure a*

2. Sew a piece C2 to the left side of each piece B, and a piece C1 to the right side, to make a unit BC, 2½″ × 4½″. Repeat to make a total of 3 units BC. *figure b*

3. Sew together units AC and BC to make 3 sets. Sew together the 3 sets AC/BC. *figure c*

Finish the Block

1. Sew pieces D to the top and bottom.

2. Sew pieces E to the left and right sides. *figure d*

figure a

figure b

figure c

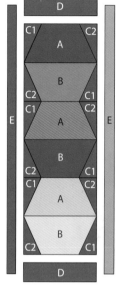

figure d

ALTERNATE IDEAS

Carpool

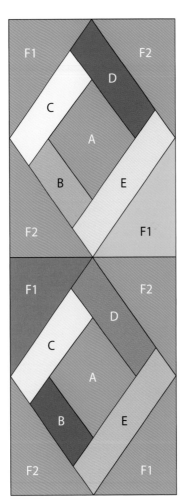

Fabric Requirements and Cutting

Piece	Number to Cut	Size to Cut	Trim Using
A	2	3″ × 4″	Template A— Pattern 32
B	2	2″ × 3½″	Template B— Pattern 32
C	2	2″ × 4¾″	Template C— Pattern 32
D	2	2″ × 4¾″	Template D— Pattern 32
E	2	2″ × 5¾″	Template E— Pattern 32
F1	4	3½″ × 4½″	Template F1— Pattern 32
F2	4	3½″ × 4½″	Template F2— Pattern 32

All seams are sewn with a ¼″ seam allowance and pressed open.

NOTE

All the pieces in this block are cut using templates from Pattern 32 (pullout page P2). The dimensions listed in the chart under "Size to Cut" represent the amount of fabric required for each piece. More fabric may be required for shortcut piecing (page 189) or fussy cutting (page 185).

To make a template from a pattern, refer to Making and Using Freezer-Paper Templates (pages 186 and 187). When cutting your fabric, remember to add seam allowances and mark points for matching seams.

Make the Block

Make the Diamond Units

1. Sew 1 each of pieces B, C, D, and E around a piece A. (This will be a lot like making a Log Cabin block, but with slightly different shapes.) *figure a*

2. Sew corner pieces F1 and F2 to the diamond to make a diamond unit 5½″ × 7½″. *figure b*

3. Repeat Steps 1 and 2 to make a second diamond unit.

4. Sew together the 2 diamond units. *figure c*

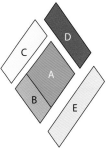

figure a

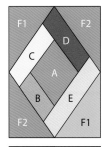

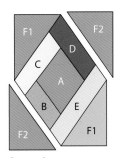

figure c

figure b

ALTERNATE IDEAS

Dog Park

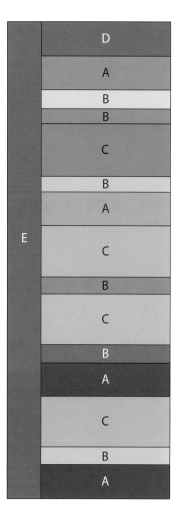

Fabric Requirements and Cutting

Piece	Number to Cut	Size to Cut
A	4	1½″ × 4½″
B	6	1″ × 4½″
C	4	2″ × 4½″
D	1	1½″ × 4½″
E	1	1½″ × 14½″

All seams are sewn with a ¼″ seam allowance and pressed open.

Make the Block

1. Sew together pieces A, B, and C as shown.

2. Sew piece D to the top of unit ABC.

3. Sew piece E to the left side of the block.

	D
	A
	B
	B
E	C
	B
	A
	C
	B
	C
	B
	A
	C
	B
	A

ALTERNATE IDEAS

Escalator

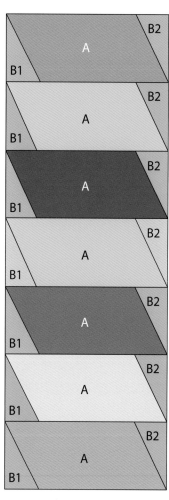

Fabric Requirements and Cutting

Piece	Number to Cut	Size to Cut	Trim Using
A	7	3″ × 6¼″	Template A— Pattern 33
B1	7	2″ × 3″	Template B1— Pattern 33
B2	7	2″ × 3″	Template B2— Pattern 33

All seams are sewn with a ¼″ seam allowance and pressed open.

--------------- **NOTE** ---------------

All the pieces in this block are cut using templates from Pattern 33 (pullout page P2). The dimensions listed in the chart under "Size to Cut" represent the amount of fabric required for each piece. More fabric may be required for shortcut piecing (page 189) or fussy cutting (page 185).

To make a template from a pattern, refer to Making and Using Freezer-Paper Templates (pages 186 and 187). When cutting your fabric, remember to add seam allowances and mark points for matching seams.

Make the Block

1. Sew a piece B1 to the left side of a piece A, and a piece B2 to the right side, to make a rectangle 2½″ × 5½″.

2. Repeat Step 1 to make a total of 7 units AB. *figure a*

3. Sew together the 7 pieced units AB. *figure b*

figure a

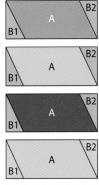

figure b

ALTERNATE IDEAS

Coffee Shop

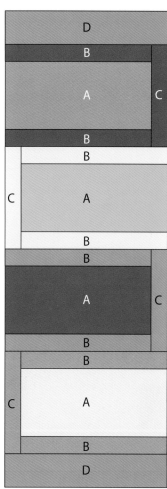

Fabric Requirements and Cutting

Piece	Number to Cut	Size to Cut
A	4	2½″ × 5″
B	8	1″ × 5″
C	4	1″ × 3½″
D	2	1½″ × 5½″

All seams are sewn with a ¼″ seam allowance and pressed open.

Make the Block

1. Sew 2 pieces B to the top and bottom of a piece A.

2. Repeat Step 1 to create a total of 4 units AB.

3. Arrange the 4 pieced units in a column. The units are numbered from 1 to 4, starting at the top.

4. Sew pieces C to the right sides of units 1 and 3. Sew pieces C to the left sides of units 2 and 4. *figures a & b*

Finish the Block

1. Sew together the 4 units ABC.

2. Sew pieces D to the top and bottom. *figure c*

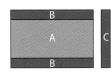
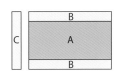

figure a

figure b

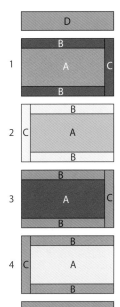

figure c

ALTERNATE IDEAS

Haircut

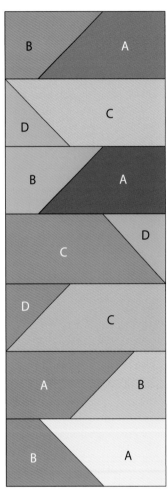

Fabric Requirements and Cutting

Piece	Number to Cut	Size to Cut
A	4	2½″ × 4½″
B	4	2½″ × 3½″
C	3	2½″ × 5½″
D	3	2½″ × 2½″

All seams are sewn with a ¼″ seam allowance and pressed open.

─────── **SEWING DIAGONAL SEAMS** ───────

Align the 2 pieces of fabric with right sides together. Use a fabric marker to draw the diagonal seam line as shown in the diagram. Sew along the marked line. Trim away the excess fabric to leave a ¼″ seam allowance. Press the seam open.

Make the Block

Make the Rows

For all rows, refer to Sewing Diagonal Seams (above).

1. Rows 1 and 3: Place a piece B on top of a piece A. Mark and sew the diagonal seam. Repeat to make a total of 2 units. *figures a & c*

2. Row 2: Place a piece D on top of a piece C. Mark and sew the diagonal seam. *figure b*

3. Row 4: Place a piece D on top of a piece C. Mark and sew the diagonal seam. *figure d*

4. Row 5: Place a piece D on top of a piece C. Mark and sew the diagonal seam. *figure e*

5. Row 6: Place a piece B on top of a piece A. Mark and sew the diagonal seam. *figure f*

6. Row 7: Place a piece B on top of a piece A. Mark and sew the diagonal seam. *figure g*

Finish the Block

Arrange rows 1–7 in a column and sew together.

figure a

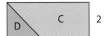
1

figure b

2

figure c

3

figure d

4

figure e

5

figure f
6

figure g
7

ALTERNATE IDEAS

Skylight

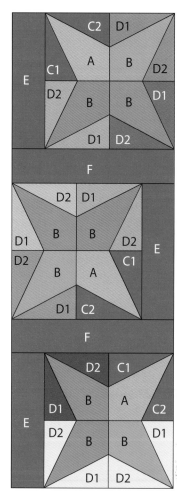

Fabric Requirements and Cutting

Piece	Number to Cut	Size to Cut	Trim Using
A	3	2¼″ × 4¼″	Template A— Pattern 34
B	9	2¼″ × 4¼″	Template B— Pattern 34
C1	3	2¼″ × 3¾″	TemplateC1— Pattern 34
C2	3	2¼″ × 3¾″	Template C2— Pattern 34
D1	9	2¼″ × 3¾″	Template D1— Pattern 34
D2	9	2¼″ × 3¾″	Template D2— Pattern 34
E	3	1½″ × 4½″	
F	2	1½″ × 5½″	

All seams are sewn with a ¼″ seam allowance and pressed open.

─────── **NOTE** ───────

Most of the pieces in this block are cut using templates from Pattern 34 (pullout page P2). The dimensions listed in the chart under "Size to Cut" represent the amount of fabric required for each piece. More fabric may be required for shortcut piecing (page 189) or fussy cutting (page 185).

To make a template from a pattern, refer to Making and Using Freezer-Paper Templates (pages 186 and 187). When cutting your fabric, remember to add seam allowances and mark points for matching seams.

Make the Block

Make the Point Units

1. Sew pieces C1 and C2 to pieces A to make 3 contrasting point units, 2½˝ × 2½˝ each. *figure a*

2. Sew pieces D1 and D2 to pieces B to make 9 point units, 2½˝ × 2½˝ each. *figure b*

Make the Star Units

Sew together 3 point units and 1 contrasting point unit to make a star unit. Repeat to make 3 star units. *figure c*

Finish the Block

1. Arrange the 3 star units in a column. Sew pieces E to the left sides of the top and bottom star units.

2. Sew the remaining piece E to the right side of the middle star unit.

3. Sew together the star units, sewing pieces F between them. *figure d*

figure a

figure b

figure c

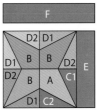

figure d

ALTERNATE IDEAS

Storefront

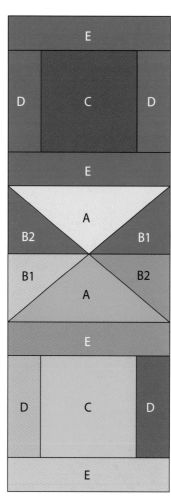

Fabric Requirements and Cutting

Piece	Number to Cut	Size to Cut	Trim Using
A	2	3″ × 6″	Template A—Pattern 35
B1	2	3¼″ × 3½″	Template B1—Pattern 35
B2	2	3¼″ × 3½″	Template B2—Pattern 35
C	2	3½″ × 3½″	
D	4	1½″ × 3½″	
E	4	1½″ × 5½″	

All seams are sewn with a ¼″ seam allowance and pressed open.

NOTE

Some of the pieces in this block are cut using templates from Pattern 35 (pullout page P2). The dimensions listed in the chart under "Size to Cut" represent the amount of fabric required for each piece. More fabric may be required for shortcut piecing (page 189) or fussy cutting (page 185).

To make a template from a pattern, refer to Making and Using Freezer-Paper Templates (pages 186 and 187). When cutting your fabric, remember to add seam allowances and mark points for matching seams.

Make the Block

1. Sew pieces B1 and B2 to the pieces A to make 2 units AB. *figure a*

2. Sew pieces D to the sides of the pieces C to make 2 units CD. Sew pieces E to the top and bottom of each unit CD. *figure b*

3. Sew a unit AB to the bottom of a unit CDE to make the top half of the block.

4. Sew a unit AB to the top of a unit CDE to make the bottom half of the block.

5. Sew together the top and bottom halves. *figure c*

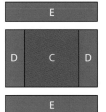

figure a

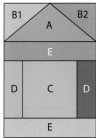

figure b

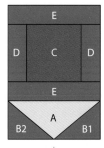

figure c

ALTERNATE IDEAS

Bookstore

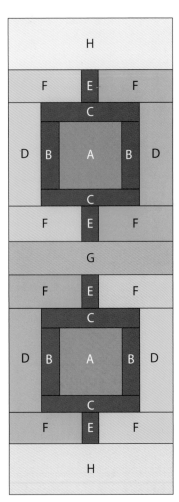

Fabric Requirements and Cutting

Piece	Number to Cut	Size to Cut
A	2	2½″ × 2½″
B	4	1″ × 2½″
C	4	1″ × 3½″
D	4	1½″ × 3½″
E	4	1″ × 1½″
F	8	1½″ × 2¾″
G	1	1½″ × 5½″
H	2	2″ × 5½″

All seams are sewn with a ¼″ seam allowance and pressed open.

Make the Block

1. Sew pieces B to the left and right sides of a piece A.

2. Sew pieces C to the top and bottom of unit AB.

3. Sew pieces D to the left and right sides of unit ABC. *figure a*

4. Repeat Steps 1–3 to make a second unit ABCD.

5. Sew pieces F to the left and right sides of a piece E.

6. Repeat Step 5 to make a total of 4 units EF. *figure b*

7. Sew units EF to the top and bottom of each unit ABCD to make 2 square units 5½″ × 5½″. *figure c*

Finish the Block

1. Sew together the units ABCDEF, sewing piece G between them.

2. Sew pieces H to the top and bottom. *figure d*

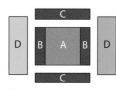
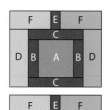

figure a

figure b

figure c

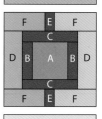
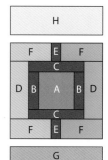

figure d

ALTERNATE IDEAS

Look Both Ways

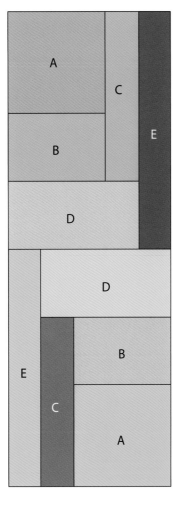

Fabric Requirements and Cutting

Piece	Number to Cut	Size to Cut
A	2	3½″ × 3½″
B	2	2½″ × 3½″
C	2	1½″ × 5½″
D	2	2½″ × 4½″
E	2	1½″ × 7½″

All seams are sewn with a ¼″ seam allowance and pressed open.

Make the Block

Make the Top Half

1. Sew a piece B to the bottom of a piece A.

2. Sew a piece C to the right side.

3. Sew a piece D to the bottom.

4. Sew a piece E to the right side. *figure a*

Make the Bottom Half

1. Sew a piece B to the top of the remaining piece A.

2. Sew a piece C to the left side.

3. Sew a piece D to the top.

4. Sew a piece E to the left side. *figure b*

Finish the Block

Sew together the top and bottom halves. *figure c*

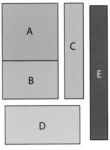
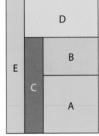

figure a

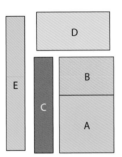

figure b

figure c

ALTERNATE IDEAS _____

Auditorium

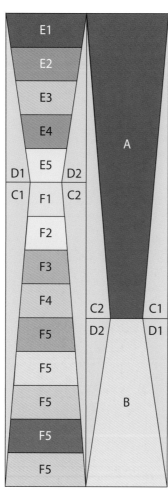

Fabric Requirements and Cutting

Piece	Number to Cut	Size to Cut	Trim Using
A	1	3½″ × 10″	Template A—Pattern 36
B	1	3½″ × 6″	Template B—Pattern 37
C1	2	1¾″ × 10½″	Template C1—Pattern 36
C2	2	1¾″ × 10½″	Template C2—Pattern 36
D1	2	2″ × 6″	Template D1—Pattern 37
D2	2	2″ × 6″	Template D2—Pattern 37
E1	1	1½″ × 3½″	
E2	1	1½″ × 3¼″	
E3	1	1½″ × 2¾″	
E4	1	1½″ × 2½″	
E5	1	1½″ × 2¼″	
F1	1	1½″ × 2¼″	
F2	1	1½″ × 2½″	
F3	1	1½″ × 2¾″	
F4	1	1½″ × 3¼″	
F5	5	1½″ × 3½″	

All seams are sewn with a ¼″ seam allowance and pressed open.

NOTE

Some of the pieces in this block are cut using templates from Patterns 36 and 37 (pullout page P1). The dimensions listed in the chart under "Size to Cut" represent the amount of fabric required for each piece. More fabric may be required for shortcut piecing (page 189) or fussy cutting (page 185).

To make a template from a pattern, refer to Making and Using Freezer-Paper Templates (pages 186 and 187). When cutting your fabric, remember to add seam allowances and mark points for matching seams.

Make the Block

Make the Right Half

1. Sew pieces C1 and C2 to piece A.

2. Sew pieces D1 and D2 to piece B.

3. Sew together the 2 pieced units. *figure a*

Make the Left Half

1. Center and sew together pieces E1–E5. Use Template E from Pattern 37 to cut unit E from the pieced unit. *figure b*

2. Center and sew together pieces F1–F5. Use Template F from Pattern 36 to cut unit F from the pieced unit. *figure c*

3. Sew pieces D1 and D2 to unit E.

4. Sew pieces C1 and C2 to unit F.

5. Sew together the 2 pieced units. *figure d*

Finish the Block

Sew together the left and right halves. *figure e*

ALTERNATE IDEAS _____

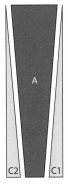

figure a

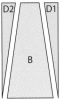

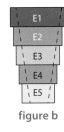

figure b

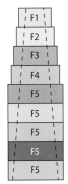

figure c

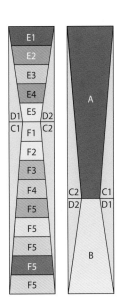

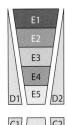

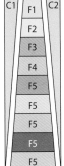

figure d

figure e

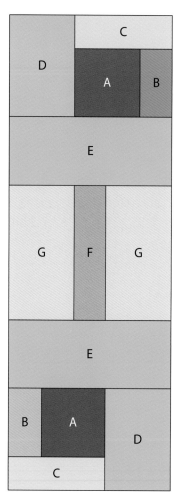

Fabric Requirements and Cutting

Piece	Number to Cut	Size to Cut
A	2	2½″ × 2½″
B	2	1½″ × 2½″
C	2	1½″ × 3½″
D	2	2½″ × 3½″
E	2	2½″ × 5½″
F	1	1½″ × 4½″
G	2	2½″ × 4½″

All seams are sewn with a ¼″ seam allowance and pressed open.

Make the Block

Make the Top Unit

1. Sew a piece B to the right side of a piece A.

2. Sew a piece C to the top.

3. Sew a piece D to the left side.

4. Sew a piece E to the bottom. *figure a*

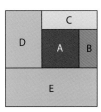

figure a

Make the Bottom Unit

1. Sew piece B to the left side of the remaining piece A.

2. Sew piece C to the bottom.

3. Sew piece D to the right side.

4. Sew piece E to the top. *figure b*

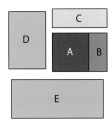
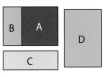

figure b

Finish the Block

1. Sew pieces G to piece F.

2. Sew the top and bottom units to unit FG. *figure c*

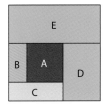

figure c

ALTERNATE IDEAS _____

Window Washer

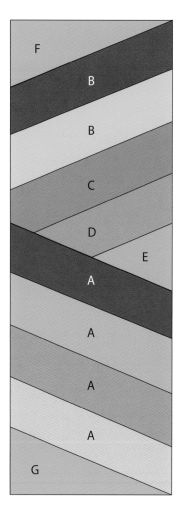

Fabric Requirements and Cutting

Piece	Number to Cut	Size to Cut	Trim Using
A	4	2″ × 7¼″	Template A—Pattern 38
B	2	2″ × 7¼″	Template B—Pattern 39
C	1	2″ × 7¼″	Template C—Pattern 39
D	1	2″ × 6″	Template D—Pattern 39
E	1	3″ × 3½″	Template E—Pattern 39
F	1	3″ × 6″	Template F—Pattern 39
G	1	3″ × 6″	Template G—Pattern 38

All seams are sewn with a ¼″ seam allowance and pressed open.

NOTE

All the pieces in this block are cut using templates from Patterns 38 and 39 (pullout page P2). The dimensions listed in the chart under "Size to Cut" represent the amount of fabric required for each piece. More fabric may be required for shortcut piecing (page 189) or fussy cutting (page 185).

To make a template from a pattern, refer to Making and Using Freezer-Paper Templates (pages 186 and 187). When cutting your fabric, remember to add seam allowances and mark points for matching seams.

Make the Block

1. Sew together pieces B, C, D, E, and F to make the top unit. *figure a*

2. Sew together pieces A and G to make the bottom unit. *figure b*

3. Sew together the top and bottom units. *figure c*

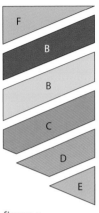

figure a

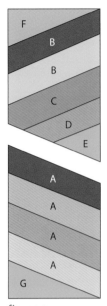

figure c

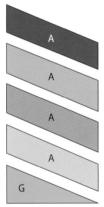

figure b

ALTERNATE IDEAS

Cornerstone

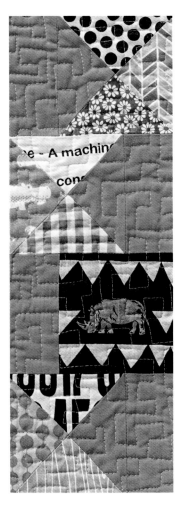

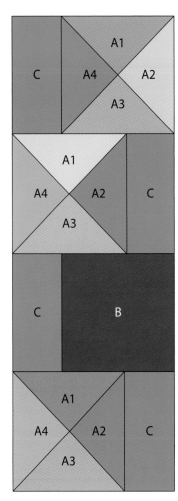

Fabric Requirements and Cutting

Piece	Number to Cut	Size to Cut	Trim Using
A1	3	3″ × 4½″	Template A1—Pattern 40
A2	3	3″ × 4½″	Template A2—Pattern 40
A3	3	3″ × 4½″	Template A3—Pattern 40
A4	3	3″ × 4½″	Template A4—Pattern 40
B	1	4″ × 4″	
C	4	2″ × 4″	

All seams are sewn with a ¼″ seam allowance and pressed open.

NOTE

Most of the pieces in this block are cut using templates from Pattern 40 (pullout page P2). The dimensions listed in the chart under "Size to Cut" represent the amount of fabric required for each piece. More fabric may be required for shortcut piecing (page 189) or fussy cutting (page 185).

To make a template from a pattern, refer to Making and Using Freezer-Paper Templates (pages 186 and 187). When cutting your fabric, remember to add seam allowances and mark points for matching seams.

Make the Block

Make the Hourglass Units

1. Sew together a piece A1 and a piece A2.

2. Sew together a piece A3 and a piece A4.

3. Sew together units A1A2 and A3A4 to make an hourglass unit A, 4″ × 4″. Repeat Steps 1–3 to make a total of 3 hourglass units. *figure a*

Make the Rows

1. Sew a piece C to the left side of an hourglass unit to make row 1.

2. Sew a piece C to the right side of an hourglass unit to make row 2.

3. Sew a piece C to the left side of piece B to make row 3.

4. Sew the remaining piece C to the right side of the remaining hourglass unit to make row 4.

Finish the Block

Sew together the 4 rows. *figure b*

ALTERNATE IDEAS _____

figure a

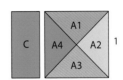

figure b

Stadium

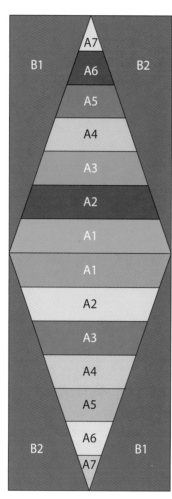

Fabric Requirements and Cutting

Piece	Number to Cut	Size to Cut	Trim Using
A1	2	1½″ × 6¼″	
A2	2	1½″ × 5¼″	
A3	2	1½″ × 4½″	
A4	2	1½″ × 4″	
A5	2	1½″ × 3¼″	
A6	2	1½″ × 2½″	
A7	2	1½″ × 1¾″	
B1	2	3½″ × 8″	Template B1—Pattern 41
B2	2	3½″ × 8″	Template B2—Pattern 41

All seams are sewn with a ¼″ seam allowance and pressed open.

NOTE

Some of the pieces in this block are cut using templates from Pattern 41 (pullout page P2). The dimensions listed in the chart under "Size to Cut" represent the amount of fabric required for each piece. More fabric may be required for shortcut piecing (page 189) or fussy cutting (page 185).

To make a template from a pattern, refer to Making and Using Freezer-Paper Templates (pages 186 and 187). When cutting your fabric, remember to add seam allowances and mark points for matching seams.

Make the Block

Make the Top Half

1. Center and sew together pieces A1–A7. Use Template A from Pattern 31 to cut unit A from the pieced unit. *figure a*

2. Sew pieces B1 and B2 to the sides of unit A.

Make the Bottom Half

1. Center and sew together pieces A1–A7. Use Template A from Pattern 31 to cut unit A from the pieced unit. *figure b*

2. Sew pieces B1 and B2 to the sides of unit A.

Finish the Block

Sew together the top and bottom halves. *figure c*

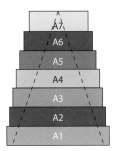
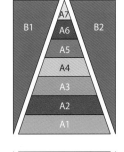
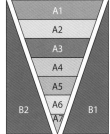

figure a

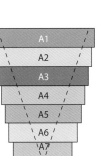

figure b

figure c

ALTERNATE IDEAS

Restaurant

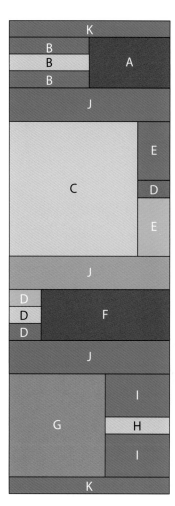

Fabric Requirements and Cutting

Piece	Number to Cut	Size to Cut
A	1	2″ × 3″
B	3	1″ × 3″
C	1	4½″ × 4½″
D	4	1″ × 1½″
E	2	1½″ × 2¼″
F	1	2″ × 4½″
G	1	3½″ × 3½″
H	1	1″ × 2½″
I	2	1¾″ × 2½″
J	3	1½″ × 5½″
K	2	1″ × 5½″

All seams are sewn with a ¼″ seam allowance and pressed open.

Make the Block

Make the Units

1. Sew together pieces B.

2. Sew piece A to the right side to make unit 1. *figure a*

3. Sew pieces E to a piece D.

4. Sew piece C to the left side to make unit 2. *figure b*

5. Sew together the remaining pieces D.

6. Sew piece F to the right side to make unit 3. *figure c*

7. Sew pieces I to piece H.

8. Sew piece G to the left side to make unit 4. *figure d*

Finish the Block

1. Sew together the 4 pieced units, sewing pieces J between each unit.

2. Sew pieces K to the top and bottom. *figure e*

ALTERNATE IDEAS _____

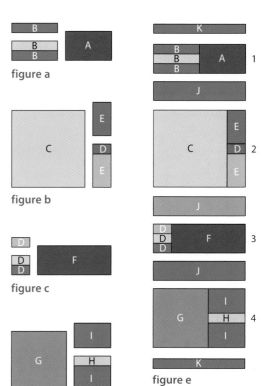

figure a

figure b

figure c

figure d

figure e

Corrugated Cardboard

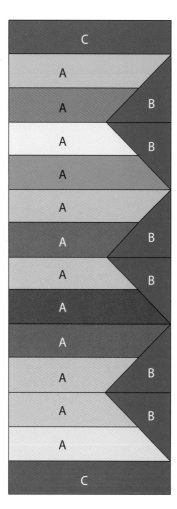

Fabric Requirements and Cutting

Piece	Number to Cut	Size to Cut
A	12	1½″ × 5½″
B	6	2½″ × 2½″
C	2	1½″ × 5½″

All seams are sewn with a ¼″ seam allowance and pressed open.

SEWING DIAGONAL SEAMS

Align the 2 pieces of fabric with right sides together. Use a fabric marker to draw the diagonal seam line as shown in the diagram. Sew along the marked line. Trim away the excess fabric to leave a ¼″ seam allowance. Press the seam open.

Make the Block

Make the Units

For Steps 2 and 3, refer to Sewing Diagonal Seams (page 146).

1. Sew together 2 pieces A. Repeat to make 6 units A. *figure a*

2. Place a piece B on top of a unit A. Mark and sew the diagonal seam. Repeat to make 3 units AB1. *figure b*

3. Place a piece B on top of a unit A. Mark and sew the diagonal seam. Note that this seam is the mirror image of the one in Step 2. Repeat to make 3 units AB2. *figure c*

Finish the Block

1. Alternate and sew together units AB1 and AB2.

2. Sew pieces C to the top and bottom. *figure d*

ALTERNATE IDEAS _____

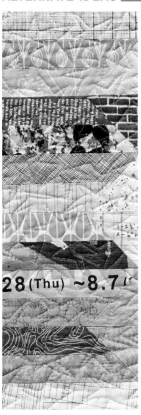

figure a

figure b

figure c

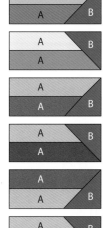

figure d

Tiki Bar

 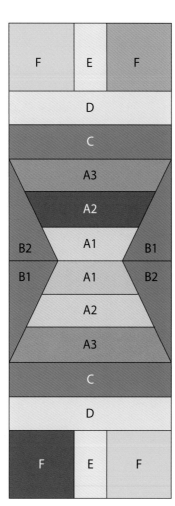

Fabric Requirements and Cutting

Piece	Number to Cut	Size to Cut	Trim Using
A1	2	1½″ × 4″	
A2	2	1½″ × 5″	
A3	2	1½″ × 6½″	
B1	2	2½″ × 4″	Template B1—Pattern 42
B2	2	2½″ × 4″	Template B2—Pattern 42
C	2	1½″ × 5½″	
D	2	1½″ × 5½″	
E	2	1½″ × 2½″	
F	4	2½″ × 2½″	

All seams are sewn with a ¼″ seam allowance and pressed open.

NOTE

Some of the pieces in this block are cut using templates from Pattern 42 (pullout page P2). The dimensions listed in the chart under "Size to Cut" represent the amount of fabric required for each piece. More fabric may be required for shortcut piecing (page 189) or fussy cutting (page 185).

To make a template from a pattern, refer to Making and Using Freezer-Paper Templates (pages 186 and 187). When cutting your fabric, remember to add seam allowances and mark points for matching seams.

Make the Block

1. Center and sew together 1 each of pieces A1–A3. Use Template A from Pattern 42 to cut a unit A from the pieced unit. Repeat to make a mirror image of the first unit A. *figure a*

2. Sew pieces B1 and B2 to the sides of each unit A.

3. Sew together the 2 pieced units AB. *figure b*

4. Sew pieces C to the top and bottom of units AB. *figure c*

5. Sew pieces D to the top and bottom of the joined units ABC.

6. Sew pieces F to the sides of each piece E. *figure d*

7. Sew units EF to the top and bottom of the block. *figure e*

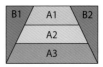

figure a

figure d

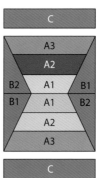

figure b

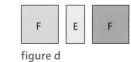

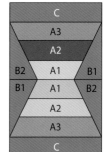

figure e

ALTERNATE IDEAS

figure c

Balcony

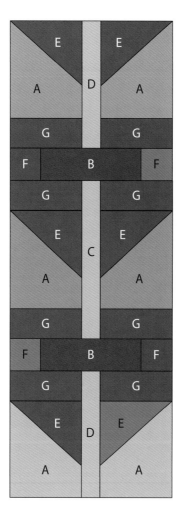

Fabric Requirements and Cutting

Piece	Number to Cut	Size to Cut
A	6	2¾″ × 3½″
B	2	1½″ × 3½″
C	1	1″ × 5″
D	2	1″ × 4¼″
E	6	2¾″ × 2¾″
F	4	1½″ × 1½″
G	8	1¼″ × 2¾″

All seams are sewn with a ¼″ seam allowance and pressed open.

——— SEWING DIAGONAL SEAMS ———

Align the 2 pieces of fabric with right sides together. Use a fabric marker to draw the diagonal seam line as shown in the diagram. Sew along the marked line. Trim away the excess fabric to leave a ¼″ seam allowance. Press the seam open.

Make the Block

Make the Leaf Units

For Steps 1 and 2, refer to Sewing Diagonal Seams (page 150).

1. Place a piece E on top of a piece A. Mark and sew the diagonal seam. Repeat to make 3 left leaf units. *figure a*

2. Place a piece E on top of a piece A. Mark and sew the diagonal seam. Repeat to make 3 right leaf units. *figure b*

Make the Top Unit

1. Sew pieces G to the bottoms of a left and a right leaf unit.

2. Sew together the 2 leaf units, sewing a stem piece D between them.

Make the Middle Unit

1. Sew pieces G to the top and bottom of a left and a right leaf unit.

2. Sew together the 2 leaf units, sewing a stem piece C between them.

Make the Bottom Unit

1. Sew pieces G to the tops of the remaining left and right leaf units.

2. Sew together the 2 leaf units, sewing a stem piece D between them.

Finish the Block

1. Sew pieces F to the sides of the pieces B. *figure c*

2. Sew together the top, middle, and bottom units, sewing units BF between them. *figure d*

figure a

figure b

figure c

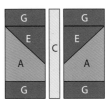

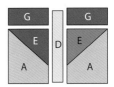

figure d

ALTERNATE IDEAS

Puddles

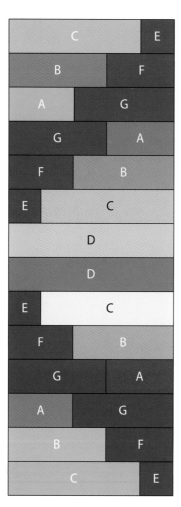

Fabric Requirements and Cutting

Piece	Number to Cut	Size to Cut
A	4	1½″ × 2½″
B	4	1½″ × 3½″
C	4	1½″ × 4½″
D	2	1½″ × 5½″
E	4	1½″ × 1½″
F	4	1½″ × 2½″
G	4	1½″ × 3½″

All seams are sewn with a ¼″ seam allowance and pressed open.

Make the Block

Make the Rows

1. For rows 1 and 14, sew together pieces C and E.

2. For rows 2 and 13, sew together pieces B and F.

3. For rows 3 and 12, sew together pieces A and G.

4. For rows 4 and 11, sew together pieces G and A.

5. For rows 5 and 10, sew together pieces F and B.

6. For rows 6 and 9, sew together pieces E and C.

7. For rows 7 and 8, use pieces D.

8. Sew together the rows.

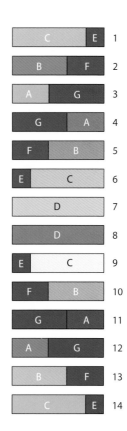

ALTERNATE IDEAS _____

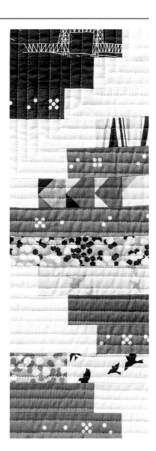

Tow-Away Zone

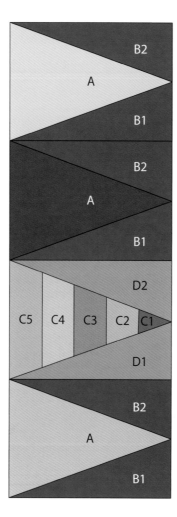

Fabric Requirements and Cutting

Piece	Number to Cut	Size to Cut	Trim Using
A	3	4½″ × 6″	Template A— Pattern 43
B1	3	3″ × 6″	Template B1— Pattern 43
B2	3	3″ × 6″	Template B2— Pattern 43
C1	1	1¾″ × 1¾″	
C2	1	1½″ × 2½″	
C3	1	1½″ × 3¼″	
C4	1	1½″ × 4″	
C5	1	1½″ × 4½″	
D1	1	3″ × 6″	Template D1— Pattern 43
D2	1	3″ × 6″	Template D2— Pattern 43

All seams are sewn with a ¼″ seam allowance and pressed open.

─────────── **NOTE** ───────────

Most of the pieces in this block are cut using templates from Pattern 43 (pullout page P2). The dimensions listed in the chart under "Size to Cut" represent the amount of fabric required for each piece. More fabric may be required for shortcut piecing (page 189) or fussy cutting (page 185).

To make a template from a pattern, refer to Making and Using Freezer-Paper Templates (pages 186 and 187). When cutting your fabric, remember to add seam allowances and mark points for matching seams.

Make the Block

1. Sew a piece B2 to the top of a piece A. Sew a piece B1 to the bottom of piece A.

2. Repeat Step 1 to make a total of 3 units AB, each 4˝ × 5½˝. *figure a*

3. Center and sew together pieces C1–C5. Use Template C from Pattern 43 to cut unit C from the pieced unit. *figure b*

4. Sew a piece D2 to the top of unit C, and a piece D1 to the bottom. *figure c*

5. Sew together units AB and CD. *figure d*

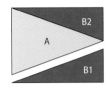
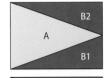

figure a

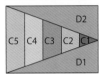

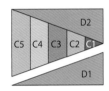

figure b

figure c

figure d

ALTERNATE IDEAS

Laundromat

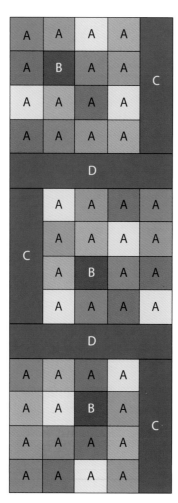

Fabric Requirements and Cutting

Piece	Number to Cut	Size to Cut
A	45	1½″ × 1½″
B	3	1½″ × 1½″
C	3	1½″ × 4½″
D	2	1½″ × 5½″

All seams are sewn with a ¼″ seam allowance and pressed open.

Make the Block

Make the Top Unit

1. Arrange a piece B and 15 pieces A in 4 rows, as shown.

2. Sew together the squares in each row. Sew the rows together.

3. Sew a piece C to the right side.

Make the Middle Unit

1. Arrange a piece B and 15 pieces A in 4 rows, as shown.

2. Sew together the squares in each row. Sew the rows together.

3. Sew a piece C to the left side.

Make the Bottom Unit

1. Arrange the remaining piece B and 15 pieces A, as shown.

2. Sew together the squares in each row. Sew the rows together.

3. Sew the remaining piece C to the right side.

Finish the Block

Sew together the top, middle, and bottom units, sewing pieces D between them.

ALTERNATE IDEAS

Do Not Enter

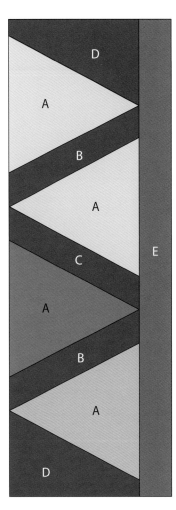

Fabric Requirements and Cutting

Piece	Number to Cut	Size to Cut	Trim Using
A	4	5¼″ × 6″	Template A—Pattern 44
B	2	1¾″ × 7″	Template B—Pattern 44
C	1	1¾″ × 7″	Template C—Pattern 44
D	2	3½″ × 6″	Template D—Pattern 44
E	1	1½″ × 14½″	

All seams are sewn with a ¼″ seam allowance and pressed open.

NOTE

Most of the pieces in this block are cut using templates from Pattern 44 (pullout page P2). The dimensions listed in the chart under "Size to Cut" represent the amount of fabric required for each piece. More fabric may be required for shortcut piecing (page 189) or fussy cutting (page 185).

To make a template from a pattern, refer to Making and Using Freezer-Paper Templates (pages 186 and 187). When cutting your fabric, remember to add seam allowances and mark points for matching seams.

Make the Block

1. Sew together pieces A, B, C, and D.

2. Sew piece E to the right side of the block.

ALTERNATE IDEAS _____

Projects

Metro Area

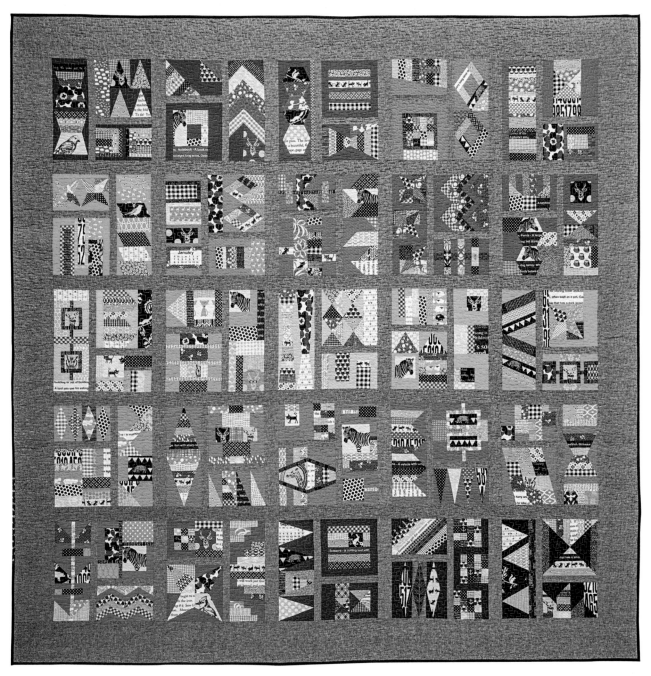

This quilt uses all 75 blocks—25 each of 5″ × 8″, 8″ × 8″, and 5″ × 14″.

If you're a quilter with a large fabric stash, making a color wheel quilt can be a fun way to compile scraps from past projects. For *Metro Area*, I started by selecting 25 different Kona Cotton solids. From there, I pulled coordinating monochromatic print fabric scraps that I contrasted with black, white, and gray prints.

Fabric Requirements

Yardages are based on fabric at least 42˝ wide.

- 4 yards neutral solid for sashing

- 8¼ yards for backing

- ¾ yard for binding

- 98˝ × 98˝ of batting

Cutting

NEUTRAL SOLID

- Cut 1 piece 90½˝ × width of fabric. Subcut:
    - 2 border strips 6½˝ × 90½˝ each
    - 2 border strips 6½˝ × 78½˝ each
    - 4 sashing strips 2½˝ × 78½˝ each

- Cut 3 strips 14½˝ × width of fabric. Subcut:
    - 20 sashing strips 2½˝ × 14½˝ each
    - 25 sashing strips 1½˝ × 14½˝ each

- Cut 1 strip 8½˝ × width of fabric. Subcut:
    - 25 sashing strips 1½˝ × 8½˝ each

BACKING FABRIC

- Cut 3 pieces 98˝ × width of fabric each.

BINDING FABRIC

- Cut 10 strips 2½˝ × width of fabric each.

Make the Block Units

All seams are sewn with a ¼″ seam allowance and pressed open.

1. Sort the 75 blocks into 25 sets, with each set including a 5″ × 8″ block, an 8″ × 8″ block, and a 5″ × 14″ block.

2. Divide the sorted blocks into 2 groups: a group of 13 sets to make 13 of block unit A, and a group of 12 sets to make 12 of block unit B.

Block Unit A

1. Beginning with a set of 3 blocks from the block unit A group, sew a 1½″ × 8½″ sashing strip to the top of the 5″ × 8″ block.

2. Sew the 8″ × 8″ block to the top of the block unit.

3. Sew a 1½″ × 14½″ sashing strip to the left side of the block unit.

4. Sew the 5″ × 14″ block to the left side of the block unit.

5. Repeat Steps 1–4 to create a total of 13 block units A. *figures a & b*

Block Unit B

1. Beginning with a set of 3 blocks from the block unit B group, sew a 1½″ × 8½″ sashing strip to the bottom of the 5″ × 8″ block.

2. Sew the 8″ × 8″ block to the bottom of the block unit.

3. Sew a 1½″ × 14½″ sashing strip to the right side of the block unit.

4. Sew the 5″ × 14″ block to the right side of the block unit.

5. Repeat Steps 1–4 to create a total of 12 block units B. *figures c & d*

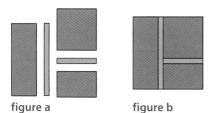

figure a   figure b

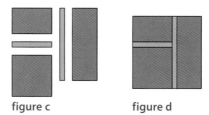

figure c   figure d

Make the Quilt Top

1. Arrange the block units in 5 rows of 5 units each, alternating the block units A and B in a checkerboard pattern. Block unit A should be in each of the 4 corners.

2. Sew together the 5 block units in each row, sewing 2½″ × 14½″ sashing strips between the block units.

3. Sew together the 5 rows, sewing 2½″ × 78½″ sashing strips between the rows.

4. Sew a 6½″ × 78½″ border strip to each side of the quilt top.

5. Sew the 6½″ × 90½″ border strips to the top and bottom of the quilt top.

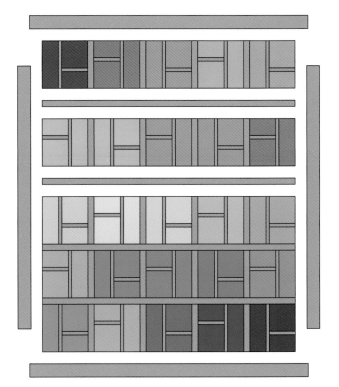

Make the Quilt Back

1. Trim away selvages. Sew together the 3 pieces along the 98″ sides.

2. Trim the finished quilt back to 98″ × 98″.

NOTE

You can add interest to your quilt back by inserting a 16″ × 98″ strip between 2 backing pieces. The added strip can be pieced from scraps and/or extra blocks. If you do that, you'll need only 5½ yards of fabric for the rest of the quilt back.

Finish the Quilt

Quilt as desired. Use the 2½″ binding strips to make and sew the binding.

I finished this quilt by free-motion quilting a continuous-line design of meandering boxes using my home machine.

Uptown

finished size: 63″ × 78″

Quilted by Krista Withers

This quilt uses 60 blocks—20 each of 5″ × 8″, 8″ × 8″, and 5″ × 14″.

Sometimes a print fabric collection is just so fabulous that it deserves its own quilt. If you want to use a single collection for your sampler, look for one that includes prints in a variety of sizes. A collection that includes monochromatic prints, multicolor prints, and some kind of picture print that can be fussy cut is ideal. *Uptown* was made using Violet Craft's Waterfront Park collection for Michael Miller.

Fabric Requirements

Yardages are based on fabric at least 42″ wide.

- 2¼ yards neutral solid for sashing

- 5 yards for backing

- ⅝ yard for binding

- 71″ × 86″ of batting

Cutting

NEUTRAL SOLID

- Cut 4 strips 2½″ × length (along the selvage edge) of fabric. Subcut:
  2 border strips 2½″ × 74½″ each
  2 border strips 2½″ × 63½″ each

- Cut 3 strips 1½″ × length of fabric. Subcut:
  4 sashing strips 1½″ × 59½″ each

- Cut 1 strip 14½″ × length of fabric. Subcut:
  35 sashing strips 1½″ × 14½″ each

- From the remaining fabric, cut 20 sashing strips 1½″ × 8½″ each.

BACKING FABRIC

- Cut 2 pieces 86″ × width of fabric each.

BINDING FABRIC

- Cut 8 strips 2½″ × width of fabric each.

Make the Block Units

All seams are sewn with a ¼″ seam allowance and pressed open.

1. Sort the 60 blocks into 20 sets, with each set including a 5″ × 8″ block, an 8″ × 8″ block, and a 5″ × 14″ block.

2. Divide the sorted blocks into 2 groups of 10 sets each; the first group will be used to make 10 of block unit A, and the other group will be used to make 10 of block unit B.

Block Unit A

1. Beginning with a set of 3 blocks in the block unit A group, sew a 1½″ × 8½″ sashing strip to the top of the 5″ × 8″ block.

2. Sew the 8″ × 8″ block to the top of the block unit.

3. Sew a 1½″ × 14½″ sashing strip to the left side of the block unit.

4. Sew the 5″ × 14″ block to the left side of the block unit.

5. Repeat Steps 1–4 to make a total of 10 block units A. *figures a & b*

Block Unit B

1. Beginning with a set of 3 blocks in the block unit B group, sew a 1½″ × 8½″ sashing strip to the bottom of the 5″ × 8″ block.

2. Sew the 8″ × 8″ block to the bottom of the block unit.

3. Sew a 1½″ × 14½″ sashing strip to the right side of the block unit.

4. Sew the 5″ × 14″ block to the right side of the block unit.

5. Repeat Steps 1–4 to make a total of 10 block units B. *figures c & d*

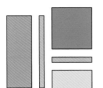

figure a   figure b

figure c   figure d

Make the Quilt Top

1. Arrange the block units in 5 rows of 4 units each, alternating block units A and B in a checkerboard pattern.

2. Sew the blocks in each row together, sewing 1½˝ × 14½˝ sashing strips between the block units.

3. Sew together the 5 rows, sewing 1½˝ × 59½˝ sashing strips between the rows.

4. Sew a 2½˝ × 74½˝ border strip to each side of the quilt top.

5. Sew the 2½˝ × 63½˝ border strips to the top and bottom of the quilt top.

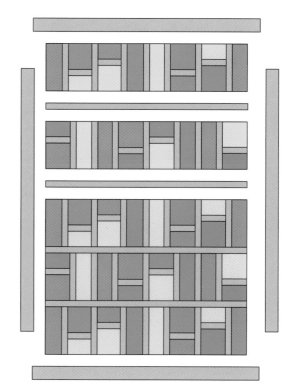

Make the Quilt Back

1. Trim away selvages. Sew together the 2 pieces along the 86˝ sides.

2. Trim the finished quilt back to 71˝ × 86˝.

─────────────── **NOTE** ───────────────
Add interest to your quilt back by making a pieced strip from your scraps and sewing it between the 2 large pieces.

Finish the Quilt

Quilt as desired. Use the 2½˝ binding strips to make and sew the binding.

This quilt was longarm quilted by Krista Withers.

Downtown

Finished size: 67″ × 67″

This quilt uses 48 blocks—16 each of 5″ × 8″, 8″ × 8″, and 5″ × 14″.

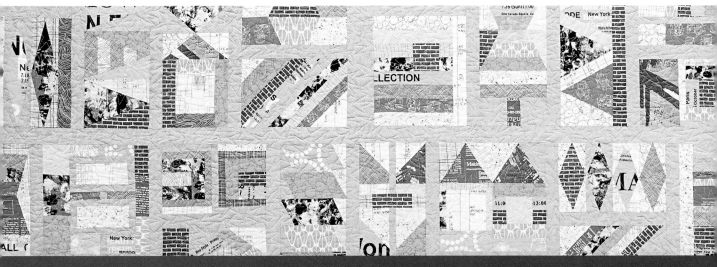

The sashing fabric on your quilt will create the negative space (or background) in which the blocks will float. The most effective sashing / negative space fabric is usually a neutral color that contrasts slightly with the fabric in the blocks.

You can further explore your quilt's negative space by including pieces of the sashing fabric in each of the blocks. This will diminish the visible block structure and cause parts of the blocks to blend into the background.

Fabric Requirements

Yardages are based on fabric at least 42″ wide.

- 2 yards neutral solid for sashing
- 4¼ yards for backing
- ⅝ yard for binding
- 75″ × 75″ of batting

Cutting

NEUTRAL SOLID

- Cut 4 strips 4½″ × length (72″ side) of fabric. Subcut:
    2 border strips 4½″ × 67½″ each
    2 border strips 4½″ × 59½″ each

- Cut 3 strips 1½″ × length of fabric. Subcut:
    3 sashing strips 1½″ × 59½″ each

- Cut 1 strip 14½″ × length of fabric. Subcut:
    28 sashing strips 1½″ × 14½″ each
    16 sashing strips 1½″ × 8½″ each

BACKING FABRIC

- Cut 2 pieces 75″ × width of fabric each.

BINDING FABRIC

- Cut 7 strips 2½″ × width of fabric each.

Make the Block Units

All seams are sewn with a ¼˝ seam allowance and pressed open.

1. Sort the 48 blocks into 16 sets, with each set including a 5˝ × 8˝ block, a 8˝ × 8˝ block, and a 5˝ × 14˝ block.

2. Divide the sorted blocks into 2 groups of 8 sets each; the first group will be used to make 8 of block unit A, and the other group will be used to make 8 of block unit B.

Block Unit A

1. Beginning with a set of blocks in the block unit A group, sew a 1½˝ × 8½˝ sashing strip to the top of the 5˝ × 8˝ block.

2. Sew the 8˝ × 8˝ block to the top of the block unit.

3. Sew a 1½˝ × 14½˝ sashing strip to the left side of the block unit.

4. Sew the 5˝ × 14˝ block to the left side of the block unit.

5. Repeat Steps 1–4 to make a total of 8 block units A. *figures a & b*

Block Unit B

1. Beginning with a set of blocks in the block unit B group, sew a 1½˝ × 8½˝ sashing strip to the bottom of the 5˝ × 8˝ block.

2. Sew the 8˝ × 8˝ block to the bottom of the block unit.

3. Sew a 1½˝ × 14½˝ sashing strip to the right side of the block unit.

4. Sew the 5˝ × 14˝ block to the right side of the block unit.

5. Repeat Steps 1–4 to make a total of 8 block units B. *figures c & d*

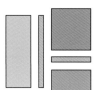

figure a

figure b

figure c

figure d

Make the Quilt Top

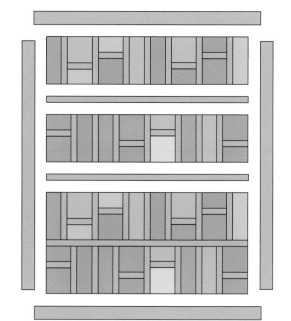

1. Arrange the block units in 4 rows of 4 block units each, alternating block units A and B in a checkerboard pattern.

2. Sew the block units in each row together, sewing 1½″ × 14½″ sashing strips between the block units.

3. Sew together the 4 rows, sewing 1½″ × 59½″ sashing strips between the rows.

4. Sew the 4½″ × 59½″ border strips to the sides of the quilt top.

5. Sew the 4½″ × 67½″ border strips to the top and bottom of the quilt top.

Make the Quilt Back

1. Trim away selvages. Sew together the 2 pieces along the 75″ sides.

2. Trim the finished quilt back to 75″ × 75″.

———————— **NOTE** ————————

Add interest to your quilt back by making a pieced strip from your scraps and sewing it between the 2 large pieces.

Finish the Quilt

Quilt as desired. Use the 2½″ binding strips to make and sew the binding.

I finished this quilt by free-motion quilting a continuous-line design of meandering points on my home machine.

Westside

Finished size: 56″ × 56″

This quilt uses all 25 of the 8″ × 8″ blocks.

Using an unexpected textile can really turn up the volume on your quilt.

Westside includes a number of print fabrics with metallic gold highlights. I continued the metallic theme by using metallic gold linen for the sashing.

Fabric Requirements

Yardages are based on fabric at least 42" wide.

- 1¾ yards neutral solid for sashing
- 3⅝ yards for backing
- ½ yard for binding
- 64" × 64" of batting

Cutting

NEUTRAL SOLID

- Cut 4 strips 4½" × length of fabric. Subcut:
    2 border strips 4½" × 56½" each
    2 border strips 4½" × 48½" each

- Cut 4 strips 2½" × length of fabric. Trim each strip to 2½" × 48½".

- From the remaining fabric, cut 20 strips 2½" × 8½" each.

BACKING FABRIC

- Cut 2 pieces 64" × width of fabric each.

BINDING FABRIC

- Cut 6 strips 2½" × width of fabric each.

Make the Quilt Top

All seams are sewn with a ¼″ seam allowance and pressed open.

1. Arrange the blocks in 5 rows of 5 blocks each.

2. Sew the blocks in each row together, sewing 2½″ × 8½″ sashing strips between the blocks. *figure a*

3. Sew the 5 rows together, sewing 2½″ × 48½″ sashing strips between the rows.

4. Sew a 4½″ × 48½″ border strip to each side of the quilt top.

5. Sew the 4½″ × 56½″ border strips to the top and bottom of the quilt top.

figure a

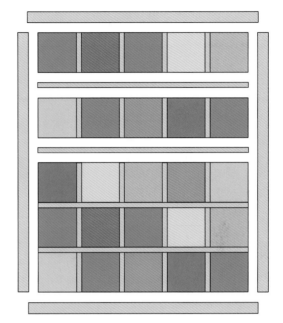

Make the Quilt Back

1. Trim away selvages. Sew together the 2 pieces along the 64″ sides.

2. Trim the finished quilt back to 64″ × 64″.

NOTE

Add interest to your quilt back by making a pieced strip from your scraps and sewing it between the 2 large pieces.

Finish the Quilt

Quilt as desired. Use the 2½″ binding strips to make and sew the binding.

I finished this quilt by free-motion quilting densely packed large, loopy flowers using my home machine.

This quilt uses all 25 of the 5″ × 8″ blocks.

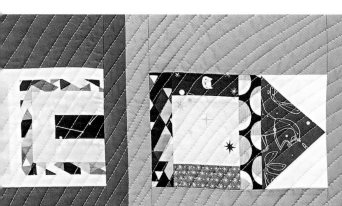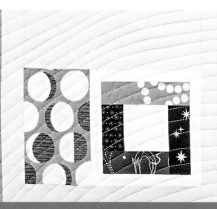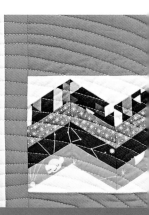

I love prints so much that I often forget about the beautiful simplicity of focusing on solid fabrics. Quilting solids are a great place to start planning a color scheme for your quilt. Using solids in your piecing can also create blocks that are bolder and more graphic than similar blocks made using only print fabrics.

Fabric Requirements

Yardages are based on fabric at least 42″ wide.

─────── **NOTE** ───────

The block backgrounds are each made with 1 piece 1½″ × 8½″, 1 piece 4½″ × 8½″, and 2 pieces 1½″ × 10½″. Yardage requirements for new fabric are provided, but don't hesitate to use whatever combination of fabrics you have on hand to make the block backgrounds!

- ¼ yard or 1 fat quarter of coordinating print fabric for 1 block background

- ⅜ yard each of 8 different coordinating solid fabrics for 24 block backgrounds

- 3½ yards for backing

- ½ yard for binding

- 58″ × 58″ of batting

Cutting

PRINT BACKGROUND FABRIC

- Cut 1 piece 1½″ × 8½″, 1 piece 4½″ × 8½″, and 2 pieces 1½″ × 10½″.

SOLID BACKGROUND FABRIC

From each of the 8 coordinating solids:

- Cut 3 pieces each of the following sizes: 1½″ × 8½″ and 4½″ × 8½″.

- Cut 6 pieces 1½″ × 10½″.

BACKING FABRIC

- Cut 2 pieces 58″ × width of fabric each.

BINDING FABRIC

- Cut 6 strips 2½″ × width of fabric each.

Make the Print Block Background

All seams are sewn with a ¼″ seam allowance and pressed open.

1. Group the cut pieces of print fabric with a block.

2. Sew the 4½″ × 8½″ piece to the top of the block.

3. Sew the 1½″ × 8½″ piece to the bottom of the block.

4. Sew the 1½″ × 10½″ pieces to the sides. *figures a & b*

Make the Solid Block Backgrounds

1. Sort the cut pieces of solid fabric into sets, with each set including the following pieces of the same fabric: 1 piece 1½″ × 8½″, 1 piece 4½″ × 8½″, and 2 pieces 1½″ × 10½″.

2. Group each set of cut pieces with a remaining block of the 24.

3. Choose a group and sew the 4½″ × 8½″ piece to the top of the block.

4. Sew the 1½″ × 8½″ piece to the bottom of the block.

5. Sew the 1½″ × 10½″ pieces to the sides.

6. Repeat Steps 3–5 with the remaining blocks to create a total of 24 block units. *figures c & d*

figure a

figure b

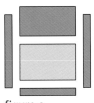

figure c

figure d

Make the Quilt Top

1. Arrange the block units into 5 rows of 5 block units each, placing the block bordered by print fabric fourth from the left in the fourth row.

2. Sew together the block units in each row. Then sew together the rows to complete the quilt top.

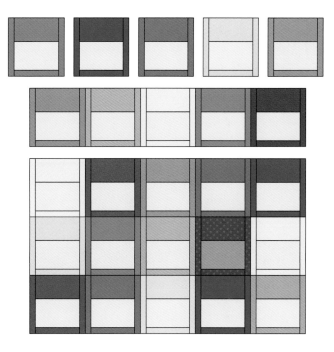

Make the Quilt Back

1. Trim away selvages. Sew together the 2 pieces along the 58˝ sides.

2. Trim the finished quilt back to 58˝ × 58˝.

———————— **NOTE** ————————

Add interest to your quilt back by making a pieced strip from scraps and sewing it between the 2 large pieces.

Finish the Quilt

Quilt as desired. Use the 2½˝ binding strips to make and sew the binding.

I finished this quilt by using my walking foot to quilt a continuous spiral design. Then I came back to where I started to finish the tighter center of the spiral using free-motion quilting.

Residential

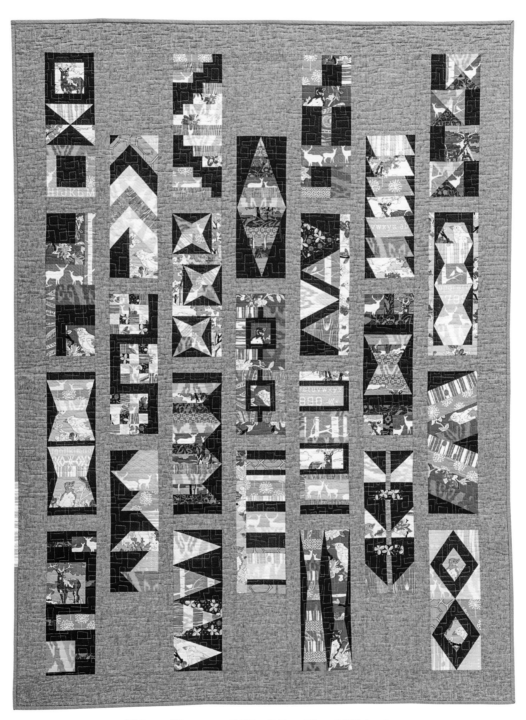

This quilt uses all 25 of the 5″ × 14″ blocks.

A sampler quilt is the perfect place to fussy cut!
Residential is full of fussy-cut deer, birds, and other images.

Fabric Requirements

Yardages are based on fabric at least 42˝ wide.

- 2 yards neutral solid for sashing

- 4¼ yards for backing

- ½ yard for binding

- 58˝ × 75˝ of batting

Cutting

NEUTRAL SOLID

- Cut 4 strips 3½˝ × length (along the selvage) of fabric. Subcut:
  2 border strips 3½˝ × 67˝ each
  2 border strips 3½˝ × 44½˝ each

- Cut 6 strips 2˝ × length of fabric. Subcut:
  6 sashing strips 2˝ × 61˝ each

- Cut 2 strips 5½˝ × length of fabric. Subcut:
  6 sashing strips 5½˝ × 8¼˝ each
  18 sashing strips 2˝ × 5½˝ each

BACKING FABRIC

- Cut 2 pieces 75˝ × width of fabric each.

BINDING FABRIC

- Cut 6 strips 2½˝ × width of fabric each.

Make the Quilt Top

All seams are sewn with a ¼″ seam allowance and pressed open.

Arrange the 25 blocks in 7 columns. Columns 1, 3, 5, and 7 each include 4 blocks. Columns 2, 4, and 6 each include 3 blocks.

Make Columns 1, 3, 5, and 7

Sew together the blocks in each column, sewing 2″ × 5½″ sashing strips between the blocks. *figure a*

Make Columns 2, 4, and 6

1. Sew together the blocks in each column, sewing 2″ × 5½″ sashing strips between the blocks.

2. Sew 5½″ × 8¼″ sashing strips to the top and bottom of each column. *figure b*

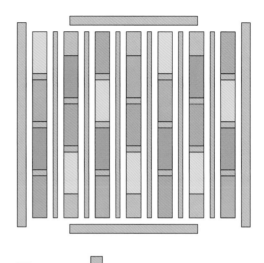

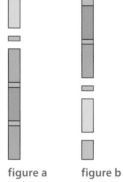

figure a   figure b

Finish the Quilt Top

1. Sew the columns together, sewing 2″ × 61″ sashing strips between the columns.

2. Sew the 3½″ × 44½″ border strips to the top and bottom of the quilt top.

3. Sew the 3½″ × 67″ border strips to the sides of the quilt top.

Make the Quilt Back

1. Trim away selvages. Sew together the 2 pieces along the 75″ sides.

2. Trim the finished quilt back to 58″ × 75″.

——————————— **NOTE** ———————————

Add interest to your quilt back by making a pieced strip from scraps and sewing it between the 2 large pieces.

Finish the Quilt

Quilt as desired. Use the 2½″ binding strips to make and sew the binding.

I finished this quilt by free-motion quilting a continuous-line design of intersecting boxes using my home machine.

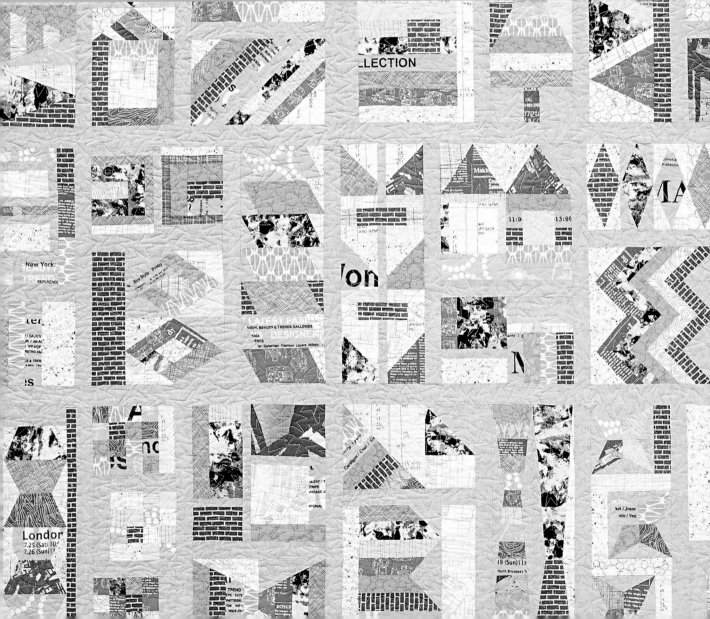

How-To

Supplies

Stock your sewing area with the following basic supplies, most of which are available at quilt shops and larger craft-supply stores.

- 45mm or 60mm rotary cutter with an ergonomic squeeze handle
- 24″ × 36″ self-healing cutting mat
- 6″ × 24″ clear plastic quilting ruler with both grid and angled markings
- 4″ × 14″ or 6″ × 12″ ruler for working with smaller pieces
- Iron and pressing board
- Starch alternative, such as Flatter smoothing spray by Soak
- Sewing machine needles: 80/12 microtex/sharp for piecing
- Long, sharp quilting pins
- Magnetic pincushion
- Fabric scissors
- Utility scissors for cutting templates
- Seam ripper and snips
- Water-soluble fabric marker
- Freezer paper for making templates (either the 8½″ × 11″ printable sheets that are available at quilt shops or the larger rolls sold in supermarkets)
- Pencil for tracing template patterns
- Envelopes for storing templates

Cutting Basics

As you look through the blocks and read the instructions, you'll find that I cut out a lot of pieces individually rather than using shortcut techniques like strip piecing. I've chosen to make my blocks and write the instructions this way not because I'm unfamiliar with these techniques but because they don't provide the same opportunities for thoughtful fabric placement. It may take longer to fussy cut a quarter-square triangle unit, but it will definitely be more beautiful and memorable!

Rotary Cutting

Accurate rotary cutting will improve the success of your projects. Make sure your fabric is free from wrinkles before you start cutting, and always use a sharp blade.

MAKING ANGLED CUTS

Most 6″ × 24″ rulers include guidelines for cutting 30°, 45°, and 60° angles. To use these guidelines, tilt the ruler to the left until the guide you want is lined up with the bottom edge of your fabric. Then cut along the side of the ruler, just as you would if you were making a standard 90° cut.

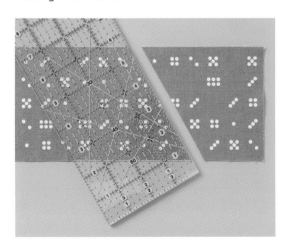

NOTE

If you are left-handed, tilt your ruler to the right, so it looks like a mirror image of the photo. This will allow you to cut safely along the left side of the ruler.

FUSSY CUTTING

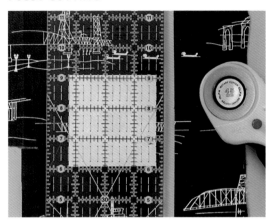

Fussy cutting is the common term for cutting a print fabric to highlight or center a particular part of the print. For this book, I recommend using freezer paper to measure fussy-cut shapes. If the block construction makes use of freezer-paper templates, you can use the templates themselves.

For the other patterns, you can use a piece of freezer paper cut to the *finished* size of the piece you want to cut. Use your iron to fuse the freezer-paper shape onto the area of the fabric you want to cut and then rotary cut the shape, adding the seam allowance just as you would if you were using a template pattern.

Making and Using Freezer-Paper Templates

Most of the nonrectangular shapes used in this book are made with freezer-paper templates. Freezer paper is an excellent template material because it can be temporarily fused to fabric by pressing with an iron, making it easy to fussy cut and to cut accurately.

Making Templates by Tracing

Use a pencil to trace the pattern shape onto the paper (nonshiny) side of the freezer paper. Be sure to transfer all markings and the name of the pattern.

Use utility scissors or an old rotary cutter blade to cut out the template patterns, and store each template in a small envelope labeled with its block name and piece ID.

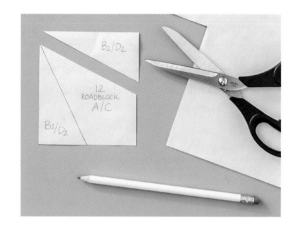

Making Templates by Printing

For your convenience, a digital file of the template patterns is available at tinyurl.com/11072-patterns-download. This file is formatted to allow printing directly onto 8½″ × 11″ freezer-paper sheets available from C&T Publishing, eliminating the need for tracing. Be sure to print onto the paper (nonshiny) side.

Use utility scissors or an old rotary cutter blade to cut out the templates, and store each one in a small envelope labeled with its block name and piece ID.

Using the Freezer-Paper Templates

The freezer-paper templates do not include seam allowances. This means that when you place the template shape onto your fabric, you can easily see what the finished shape will look like without a seam allowance, making it very easy to fussy cut. It also means that you won't inadvertently shave off bits of your template as you work.

Once you've determined where you want to cut the shape, place the template shiny side down and briefly press it with an iron. A dry iron is best, particularly if you've used an inkjet printer to print onto the freezer paper. The heat will melt the coating on the back of the paper, which will hold the template in place while you cut. (Don't worry! It will peel off when you're finished, without any damage to the fabric.)

Carefully move the fabric back to your cutting mat and use a ruler to cut the shape, adding a ¼″ seam allowance around all sides.

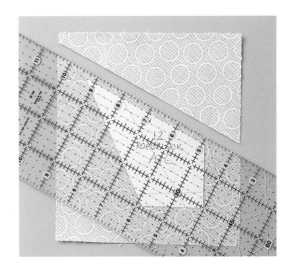

Use a water-soluble fabric marker to mark each corner or point on the fabric shape. These points will be used to match and sew the pieces accurately.

— NOTE —

Be sure to use a water-soluble, not a disappearing-ink, marker. You don't want your marks to disappear while you work!

Peel away the freezer-paper template and save it for making the next shape, or for making another block later. Freezer-paper templates won't last forever, but you should be able to cut several shapes from each one before it becomes too linty to adhere to the fabric.

Sewing Basics

Seam Allowances

The projects in this book are made using a ¼″ seam allowance. Sewing an accurate ¼″ seam allowance will help ensure that your finished blocks are the right size. To easily achieve accuracy, I recommend using a ¼″ piecing foot. I prefer the kind without the flange or guide on the side, but some quilters find it helpful.

Pressing Seams

I press my seams open. It takes a bit more effort than pressing them to one side, as many quilters do, but I think the results are worth it. If you press the seams open, your finished blocks will be more precise, will lie flatter, and will be easier to machine quilt in an allover pattern.

Having said that, I realize that many of the designs in this book involve a lot of small pieces. If you find that you're fighting with a particular seam, don't hesitate to press that seam to the side!

Sewing the Cut Shapes

Use the marked points to match the pieces to one another, keeping in mind that unlike rectangular shapes, the shapes cut from the templates may need to be lined up at what look like odd angles, rather than by simply matching the ends of the pieces.

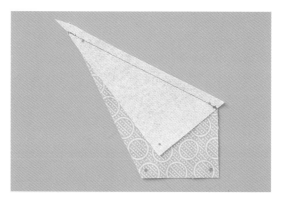

─────── **TIP** ───────

If you're having trouble lining up the marked points, try sticking a pin through the point in one piece and then through the point you are trying to match. Pull the head of the pin all the way up to the fabric, matching the points perfectly. Then use a second pin to secure them together.

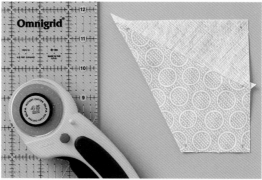

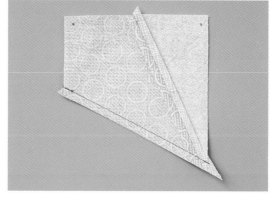

Sew the pieces together using a ¼″ seam allowance and press the seam open. Trim away any additional seam allowance (for instance, on points) before sewing more pieces. Once all the pieces have been joined, square up the block or block unit, removing any excess seam allowance.

Remove any remaining markings by blotting with a damp washcloth.

SHORTCUT PIECING

If you want to avoid matching up the tiniest template shapes and are willing to use a little more fabric, you may prefer shortcut piecing.

For this method, begin by cutting to size the first piece you need to sew, leaving the freezer-paper template fused to the fabric. Don't worry about marking the points as you would with standard piecing.

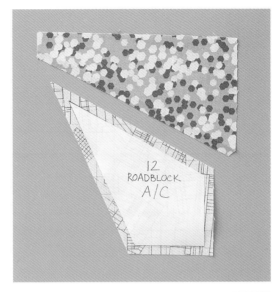

In shortcut piecing, you'll sew on the next piece of fabric before you cut it to size. This eliminates the need for matching points and fiddling with the tiniest pieces.

Refer to the block pattern to see which piece should be added next and select a piece of fabric a little larger than you think you'll need. Depending on the look you're going for and the fabric you're using, you may want to cut the fabric at a matching angle before you sew it on. Do this by using the edge of the freezer-paper template as a guide.

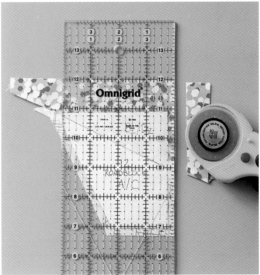

Sew the two pieces of fabric together, centering the already cut piece on the larger piece that you're adding. Press the seam open.

Use your iron to fuse the freezer-paper template in place, matching it with the freezer-paper template still on the first piece.

Use your rotary cutter and ruler to trim away the excess fabric, leaving a ¼″ seam allowance. Continue using this method to add generously cut pieces of fabric, fuse the templates in place, and cut the block components to size until all the pieces are sewn.

If you find that your freezer-paper templates are not staying fused in place or are getting caught in the seams, don't hesitate to peel them off the block during sewing. Just take a moment to fuse them back in place each time you trim to size a new part of the block.

Additional Information

Detailed explanations of quilting basics such as cutting, piecing, making a quilt sandwich, machine quilting at home, and making and sewing binding can be found in my earlier books *The Practical Guide to Patchwork* and *Modern Patchwork*. You can also refer to C&T Publishing's website for general quiltmaking instructions: ctpub.com > Resources > Consumer Resources: Quiltmaking Basics.

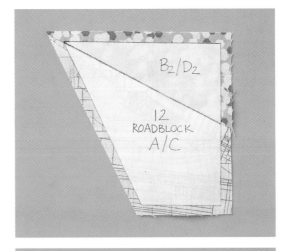

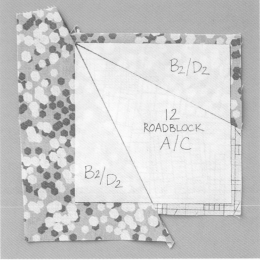

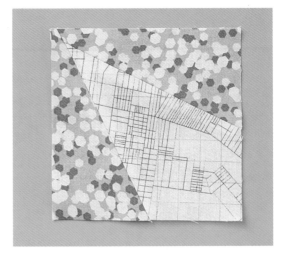

About the Author

Elizabeth Hartman is a full-time quilter, designer, and teacher from Portland, Oregon. She is the author of the best-selling quilting guide *The Practical Guide to Patchwork* and *Modern Patchwork*. Elizabeth is the author of the popular blog and pattern shop at ohfransson.com, through which she has introduced thousands of people to modern quilting.

Photo by Jen Carlton Bailly

Resources

JANOME SEWING MACHINES
Janome 1600P-QC
janome.com

I did all of my piecing and quilting on my Janome 1600P-QC. Read more about this machine at janome.com

LONGARM QUILTING SERVICES
Krista Withers Quilting
kristawithersquilting.blogspot.com

Krista did a beautiful job on my *Uptown* quilt. See more of her quilting at kristawithers.blogspot.com

I encourage everyone to support their local fabric shops! Additionally, here are a few online shops that carry fabrics like the ones I used in this book, including Robert Kaufman's Kona Cotton solids and Essex cotton/linen blends.

City Craft
citycraft.com

Fabricworm
fabricworm.com

Form and Fabric
formandfabric.com

Pink Castle Fabrics
pinkcastlefabrics.com

Pink Chalk Fabrics
pinkchalkfabrics.com

Purl Soho
purlsoho.com

Sew Modern Online
sewmodern.com

Superbuzzy
superbuzzy.com